What readers are saying about Tony and Frank Fiore's
Lean, Mean, Business Machine

Working with businesses for the past three decades has given me the opportunity to learn which ones will flourish and which ones will not survive. With "The Lean, Mean Business Machine," Tony and Frank Fiore have created a blueprint to help businesses be the ones that thrives for years to come. I highly recommend this book to any entrepreneurs looking to make the leap from merely giving themselves a job to creating a well-oiled machine that runs on its own.
—Michael Arnold, Palmetto Partners, LLC

You can learn to implement systems in your business to accomplish extraordinary things! Tony and Frank pull no punches in preparing us psychologically to do what it will take to run our small business better, faster & more efficient. Their direct approach in delivery of this relevant knowledge makes this book easy to read and understand. This book will give you not only the motivation, inspiration and vision to take your business to the next level, but also the practical knowledge and tools to organize and implement the systems needed to help you accomplish extraordinary things in your business.
—Robert Chamberland, CPA, MST, Chamberland Business Accounting

As a general rule, I don't read business books as they rarely excite me or tell me something I don't already know. However I make exceptions for a few gems such as "The E-Myth" and "Six Steps to Small Business Success." I'm adding your book to this list. I've already quoted sections of the book to several of my managers since reading it last week. If you were trying for a powerful, lean and mean approach to the topic of owning and running a small business today you've succeeded. There's no fluff in this book just a lot of truths and hard realities that business owners need to hear and hopefully incorporate into their business models. Thank you for exciting me.
—R Van Ballantyne, EA, MBA, ATP, Counting House Associates

Congratulations, Tony and Frank, on "The Lean, Mean Business Machine." You have succeeded in sharing a career worth of lessons in a short, conversational, engaging book. You have presented the material in the same way you talk. No sugar coating, not a bunch of theory, just valuable insights presented in a straightforward way. I believe you have hit the target in your discussions on founding the business, running it, growing the business and what it means to succeed. In fact, effectively applying the insights from the book could mean the difference between success and failure. In my opinion, you have created the definitive step by step guide to small business success. If I had had this book 20 years ago, the road in my business career would have been much easier. Thanks again.
—Norbert Gonzales Jr. CPA/Attorney at Law, CEO, The Gonzales Group

THE LEAN, MEAN, BUSINESS MACHINE

Other books by Tony and Frank Fiore:

Contributing authors for
Six Steps to Small Business Success

THE LEAN, MEAN, BUSINESS MACHINE

A No-Nonsense,
Hit-You-Upside-the-Head-with-a-Baseball-Bat,
Common-Sense Guide to
Running a Profitable Small Business

Tony and Frank Fiore

MAVEN
MARK
BOOKS
Milwaukee, Wisconsin

Copyright © 2014 by Tony and Frank Fiore,
and Accounting Freedom, Ltd
All rights reserved.

Published by
MavenMark Books
An imprint of HenschelHAUS Publishing, Inc.
www.henschelHAUSbooks.com

ISBN: 978159598-340-4
E-ISBN: 978159598-341-1
LCCN: 2014946113

Publisher's Cataloging-In-Publication Data
(Prepared by The Donohue Group, Inc.)

Fiore, Tony, 1956-
The lean, mean, business machine : a no-nonsense, hit-you-upside-the-
head-with-a-baseball-bat, common-sense guide to running a profitable
small business / Tony and Frank Fiore.
pages : charts ; cm
Issued also as an ebook.
ISBN: 978-1-59598-340-4
1. Small business–Management. 2. Success in business. I. Fiore,
Frank, 1985- II. Title.
HD62.7 .F56 2014658.022   2014946113

Printed in the United States of America .

This book is dedicated to our clients—
past, present, and future.

TABLE OF CONTENTS

FOREWORD

I have known and worked with Tony and Frank Fiore for over 15 years. I have witnessed their deep understanding and commitment to helping small business clients grow and prosper while achieving a balanced life.

This book focuses on the psychology behind business owners to motivate them to execute sound business practices. Business owners hit walls that prevent them from earning more while working less. This book helps them knock down these walls.

The book also discusses the importance of having in place internal operating systems that help improve profits, customer service, and referrals, while making it easier to run and monitor the business.

I have read hundreds of business books and have consulted over 1,000 business people in my career. This is by far the best book I have read in helping a business owner become motivated to improve and systemize his or her business. I highly recommend reading this book if you are in business or are thinking of going into business.

—David Lucier, CPA, CGMA, Tax CEA

INTRODUCTION

The purpose of this book is threefold.

First, to make your business more profitable by showing you how to run it properly.

Secondly, to give you more free time once your business is running properly.

Last, to give you insight and a guide to what becoming independently wealthy means.

Accomplishing these goals is not going to be easy. There literally could be hundreds of volumes written on each subject.

We know and respect that you are very busy running your business, dealing with your family, church, sports, and life in general and have little time to waste.

That is why we have chosen to write a no-nonsense, get-down-to-business, get-in-your-face type of a book...a book like no other business book you have ever read before in your life.

We have some tough love for you throughout this book, as well as no-nonsense, common-sense solutions to increase the profitability of your business, give you more free time to enjoy those increased profits, and to start you on your way to becoming independently wealthy. All three of these goals need to work hand in hand with each other.

Ask yourself these three important questions:

1. What good is having a ton of money, if you have no free time to spend or enjoy it?

2. What good is having a bunch of free time, if you can't do anything because you don't have the money?

3. What does working hard your entire life accomplish, if you don't have enough money to live independently wealthy when you retire?

Do any of these questions hit home? All three of these must be in balance. One without the other just doesn't cut it. Throughout the book, we will be addressing each of these questions.

You might be asking yourself a couple of questions. Why are Tony and Frank writing this book? Who are the author(s), and why should I listen to them? The answers are simple, but first, we should give you a little background on us, our firm, and the accounting industry in general. Then you can decide if you want to follow our advice.

We run and operate Accounting Freedom, Ltd. which has two branches, one in Mundelein, Illinois and the other in Grafton, Wisconsin. Accounting Freedom, Ltd. is a CPA firm that specializes in working with small businesses and was started in 1981 by Anthony Fiore, CPA. Tony, who is the CEO, has a Master's degree in Taxation (MST) from DePaul University in Chicago, Illinois, and a Bachelor's degree in Accounting from Northern Illinois University in DeKalb, Illinois.

Tony is also currently the co-owner and CEO of two additional companies, Payroll Specialists, Inc., which focuses on helping small businesses with all of their payroll needs, and Accountants Solutions, Inc., a software company that develops software to help accountants run their firms more profitably.

Tony has also owned numerous other companies in the past. He is also an accomplished writer. In addition to co-authoring this book, he is also a contributing author for the book, *Six Steps to Small Business Success*. He is a sought-after speaker and has presented many seminars over the past three decades, including "How to run a profitable small business," "How to start a profitable small business," "Debt-free and prosperous living," along with numerous seminars on all aspects of running a profitable accounting firm at the semi-annual conferences of the Professional Association of Small Business Accountants (PASBA). He has served on many boards and committees serving his industry and community for many years. In 2014, Accounting Freedom, Ltd. won the coveted "Accounting Firm of the Year" award at the national PASBA convention.

Frank Fiore, CPA, joined Accounting Freedom, Ltd. in 2000. Frank is president of the organization and has a Bachelor's degree in Accounting from Roosevelt University in Chicago, Illinois. He is responsible for all of the operations of Accounting Freedom, Ltd. In addition to co-authoring this book, he is also a contributing author to *Six Steps to Small Business Success*. Like his father, Tony, he is an accomplished speaker and has presented many seminars on all aspects of running a profitable accounting firm at the semi-annual conferences of the Professional Association of Small Business Accountants. Frank has also served on the Board of Directors of PASBA.

Well, that is enough of titles and accolades, because frankly, they don't mean a hill of beans when it comes to running a small business. In 1981, Tony realized that there was a niche in the marketplace for an accountant who truly specializes in, and understands, small businesses.

The dirty little secret in the accounting industry is that most of the accounting firms across the country shy away from small businesses, especially new, start-up businesses. Why? you might ask. It's because they feel that small companies are small potatoes and not worth the time and effort. Sure, they will take them on as new clients, but often treat the "little guys" like second-class citizens.

The scenario usually goes something like this. They will tell their client to use QuickBooks®, spreadsheets, or write their checks manually, and to bring the information to them in January of the following year to get their taxes done. Does that sound familiar to you?

Early on, Tony realized this approach was completely wrong. The small business owner is the one who needs good, sound business advice and on-time monthly financial statements more than anyone. For over 30 years, Accounting Freedom, Ltd. has been doing just that for its clients who will heed the advice, instead of just preparing their tax returns at the end of the year.

Good sound business advice results in a business that runs more smoothly with more profits, and more free time for the owner, which eventually can result in the owner becoming independently wealthy.

So, we've decided that after 30 years plus, it's time to hit the keyboard and start writing down the time-honored principles we have shared with our clients, helping as many small business owners as we can reach their American dream. Hence the title of the book.... *The Lean, Mean, Business Machine*.

As you read the book, page after page, we hope that you will see the light and have a REVELATION about your business, that if put into practice will absolutely increase your PROFITS.

In the first part of the book, we are going to focus on and share with you the principles of HOW to run a small business successfully.

Secondly, we are going to discuss the principle of HOW to squeeze out and maximize the profits from your small business.

Following these principles will help you accomplish the third goal of this book: living independently wealthy.

BUT....before you start reading any further, we have a warning for you......

WARNING!!!

The journey you are embarking on will not be easy and will take a lot of hard work, long hours, deep soul searching, and tremendous commitment on your part.

In fact, improving your business is a job that will NEVER end because you will always be fine-tuning the processes. If the point comes that you think you have it all completed and figured out, it will be time to hang up your cleats because you have either stopped looking or you have lost your passion. Your business, profits, and quality of life can ALWAYS be improved upon.

Take it from us...we know. Over the last 30 years, we have spent countless hours, made hundreds of mistakes, and spent hundreds of thousands of dollars in the effort to improve our own accounting practice.

The wisdom in this book is priceless and it is our wish that every business owner learn from our experience and our long journey. However, if you are thin-skinned and can't take the heat, or are hard-headed, stubborn, and not going to listen or change what you are doing, stop reading and close the book and give it to someone who will use it. If that is the case, you are too far gone to help anyway, so don't waste your time or ours.

If you think you are tough enough to take being hit upside the head with a baseball bat, will listen to no-nonsense, common-sense solutions, will take the time and invest the energy to implement them, then read on, because you have found the right book!!

—Tony and Frank Fiore

CHAPTER 1

IS IT YOUR FAULT?

Sooooo.....is it your fault?

Well, you're still here, are you?

Congratulations!! You are a tough guy or gal. Let's see if you can take it. Buckle up for the ride!!

We will ask you again: Is it your fault that your business is not the best it can be?

We can't hear you!!

Everyone either knows someone or knows of someone who has an addiction.

What are the very first things addicts need to do in order to get help? You got it. The very first things they have to do are:

1. Admit that they have a problem

2. Realize that they are the cause of the problem, and

3. Realize that they are the solution to the problem.

This is NO different. You know that you have an issue or issues with your business, so you better look into the mirror and take the first step and admit it.

Go on, don't be shy, come on and admit you have a problem.

But you must remember also. It is a problem that can be solved.

Do you feel better?

Are you going to do something about it now? Just like the addict, you and only you, are the one who can make it happen. We can talk to you until we are blue in the face, but it won't matter until you admit to yourself that you have a problem.

If your business is not going as well as you'd like or is even in distress, if you can't take it anymore and are all stressed out about all of this, there is a second thing you must admit:

IT'S 100% YOUR FAULT, and
100% YOUR RESPONSIBILTY.

Did you hear us?? Your business is your responsibility. Stop your excuses and stop blaming it on everything and everyone else....the economy, employees, your family, suppliers, the President, Congress, your brother-in-law, competition, your banker, the stock market, your neighbor, your landlord, cash flow, sales, your customers, your dog, etc., etc. The problem isn't your business, or any of these things, and it never has been.

The problem and issue is YOU!

Take control. No one is going to make it happen except you. No one can change anything to make your business or life better, except you. Now, get off your duff, quit complaining and making excuses, and get to work!

Your business is like having a baby. How many of you have kids or know of someone who does? When a baby is born, it is completely helpless and completely dependent on you. You must do everything for it.

As the baby develops, you must give it direction, you must guide it with tough love with an ultimate, main goal of having your child be self-sustaining and self-sufficient.

You know there will be major bumps in the road along the way—emotionally and financially.

Hopefully, it will never happen, but if your child got into trouble, wouldn't you do anything possible to help your child out, no matter what. You would give up your life, your finances, your time, and whatever else it took. You would do it, because it is your child.

Let us ask you a hard question. Do you feel the same way about your business?

Well, you should!!

If you don't, you had better start right now. It is your baby...you conceived it, didn't you? You must have the same strong feelings and convictions about your business that you have for your baby, or any family member for that matter.

From this point forward, there is going to be one hard, fast rule you are going to have to live by....***NO MORE EXCUSES!***

You are going to have to change your way of thinking or nothing will change in your life or in the life of your business.

We want you to do something right now. Stand up! You heard us. We said, "**Stand up!**"

Look to your left. We want you to pretend you are looking into your past, at the last five years of your life. What do you see? How far have you come? How much have you developed? How much has your income gone up? How much has your net worth gone up? How much more free time do you have to do what you want to do instead of going to work? Are you truly better off today than you were five years ago?

Now look to your right. Now pretend you are looking five years into your future. What do you see out there?

We can tell you what most people see when they look to their right. They will be seeing a mirror image of the last five years with very little progress or change in their lives or the lives of their business.

In other words...if you do what you've always done, you'll get what you've always got....duh!

Do you want to be one of those people? Well, do you? We sure don't.

We can tell you with 100% certainty—if you don't change your way of thinking about your life and your business, nothing is going to change.

Five years from now when you do the same exercise and look to your left, you will not see any difference from today and you will still be in the same exact place with the same exact, pitiful excuses! What a waste!

Remember....**IT IS 100% YOUR FAULT, and 100% YOUR RESPONSIBILITY**.

YOU are the only one that can fix it. YOU are the only one who can put yourself on the road to recovery.

What choice are you going to make today?

Here comes the bat again. If you want to change your business and your life for the better, then read on. If not, close the book, give it to someone else, and go on making the same excuses for the rest of your life.

## CHAPTER 2

WHAT DOES INDEPENDENTLY WEALTHY MEAN?

Sooooo.....what does independently wealthy mean? We'll bet it's not what you think.

We have a startling statistic for you. Do you realize that approximately 2% of the American population retires independently wealthy? Only 2%! That is pathetic. Especially since this is America, the land of opportunity!

This figure is even more startling when you understand the definition of independently wealthy. This does not by any stretch of the imagination mean mega rich.

Basically, it means that when you retire and are not working anymore, you will have the same amount of money coming in from investments each year that you had coming in from your business or a paycheck.

You will have enough money coming in so that you will not have to change your current lifestyle. You could live as you always have lived, with one important difference:

you do not have to go to work anymore!!! Wouldn't that be totally awesome?

You won't have to downsize your house, cut your expenses, stop vacationing, or drive an old beat-up car. You won't need to live off of a promised social security benefit that probably won't even be there for the majority of us.

It doesn't matter if you are currently living on $20,000 or $20 million per year, the investment income you have coming in replaces your earned income. You don't have to work anymore, and still have the same amount of money coming in. Got it?

Think about the pathetic flip side of this situation. Ninety-eight percent of Americans will NOT retire independently wealthy. They will have to completely change their lifestyles, downsize, live off of Social Security, or be dependent on family members or others.

How sad is that? Especially in America, where you have direct control of your own destiny.

You have to decide today. Your destiny is in your own hands. Are you ready to learn and make changes?

Which group are you going to fall into? Are you going to be in the 2% , living independently wealthy when you retire or the 98% of the population who are going to have to change their lifestyles dramatically to survive, and possibly have to live off of dog food?

We know what our choice is going to be. We don't know about you, but steak and lobster sound much more appealing to us than Fido's diet.

If you are with us, roll up your sleeves, get ready to rock and roll, and read on. We've told you before and we are going to tell you again—if you are not with us, don't waste your time or ours. Close this book and go on living as before, drowning in your excuses.

If you are with us, let's start to dig in and get you on the right path to a better life.

Are you ready to start working outside your business, Mr. or Ms. Expert?

Chapter 3

What's Your Expertise?

Sooooo.....what's your expertise?

We'll bet we know your answer to that question without ever hearing your response.

We'll bet you answered, "My expertise is an electrician, carpenter, dentist, doctor, computer geek, engineer, landscaper, shoe salesman, yadda, yadda, yadda."

The answer you gave is directly related to the business you opened. Come on, admit it. We were right, weren't we?

We'll make a second bet with you. We'll bet you didn't answer "Running a small business is my expertise." Were we right again? Yep, yep, yep! We were right again, weren't we?

We'll bet you a third time. We'll bet you're asking yourself some questions right now. How do these guys know me so well? Do they secretly know me? Are they following me? Am I in the *Twilight Zone?*

All kidding aside. Let's face it and be honest for a second. Small business owners usually have one major expertise. That expertise is usually their talent or the field in which they have chosen to work. That talent or field is usually why they started the business in the first place.

If you are like most small business owners, you normally don't have a clue on how to run a business and only know how to work inside of it. For the most part, you have just created a job for yourself.

For example, there is the carpenter who is excellent at building houses, the electrician who can wire up any building, the computer geek who can fix any computer problem, the mom who starts a daycare center, the barber who opens a barber shop, the accountant who starts an accounting firm—the list goes on and on.

Unfortunately, most business owners don't have a clue about RUNNING a small business. The carpenter knows how to build houses, but doesn't have a clue about how to RUN a business that builds houses. The electrician can wire a building, but doesn't have a clue on how to RUN a business that does electrical contracting. The computer geek can fix any computer, but doesn't have a clue on how to RUN a business that fixes computers.

The mom loves to watch kids, but doesn't have a clue on how to RUN a business that watches kids. The barber knows how to cut hair, but doesn't have a clue on how to RUN a business that cuts hair. The accountant who is a great accountant and can do tax returns, but doesn't have a clue on how to RUN a business that does accounting. You get the picture.

We'd like to share with you John's story. This is an actual client story. The name has been changed to protect the GUILTY party. I'll bet you thought we were going to say protect the "innocent." Nope, to the contrary—guilty is the proper term.

Unfortunately, John, as you will understand after reading the next few paragraphs, was the prosecutor, jury, and judge in his own trial. Guess what? By not changing his ways, he convicted himself to a life sentence of hard work with the reward of a firing squad waiting for him at retirement age.

John, who is a landscaper, has been a client of ours for many years. John started his business in his early 30s and is now in his 50s. John is the typical small business owner who always worked *inside* his business instead of working *outside* his business.

As you can imagine, working as a landscaper is physically demanding. Over the years, it has taken a tremendous physical toll on John's body.

For years, we have been pounding into John's head that he needs to transition out of working INSIDE his business and start working OUTSIDE his business. He needs to start to develop a business that does work as a landscaping company instead of him doing the landscaping himself.

John is an old-school, hard-headed, tough guy, and would not listen to our recommendations.

There was always an excuse not to change his ways" "I can't find reliable help." "No one can do the job as well as I can." "I can't afford it." "I can't trust anyone to be left alone at customers' businesses or homes." "I don't have the time." "I don't have the knowledge." "You guys just don't understand my business." "It can't be done!" The list went on and on.

The other day, John came into our office around 3 p.m. He slowly and painfully dropped into a chair in front of the desk and had a complete look of despair in his eyes. We asked, "So what's going on, John?"

All stressed out and with a tear in his eyes, he said. "I just can't physically do this anymore. It takes me 15 minutes to get out of bed every morning. My body is shot from head to toe. I can't do all of this heavy lifting, cutting, and digging anymore. I'm in constant pain, day and night. I'm just plain worn out physically, and burned out mentally. I'm stuck. I have a kid in a private high school and one in college so I have to keep working, but my body can't handle it. I'm not 20 years old anymore. I should have listened to you guys years ago about how to run this blasted business. Now look at where I am: close to retirement with little money and nowhere to turn, and a body that's shot."

Does John's story sound painfully familiar to you? Well it should because John is in the same boat as many, many small business owners in America.

If John's story is your story, don't despair. There is still hope for you to turn your business and your life around.

Here comes the bat again. You really need to make sure to get your head out of the spot where the sun doesn't shine if you want change to happen!

We hope that after hearing John's story, and after removing your head, you are starting to get the picture. Running a business and working OUTSIDE your business is the polar opposite of working INSIDE your business and requires an entirely different mindset, knowledge, and skills.

The lack of knowledge of how to do this is nothing to be ashamed or afraid of because you are in the same boat as the majority of small business owners out there.

If you haven't found out already, you will at some point realize that you have to wear numerous hats to run a small business.

The idea of running a business (working OUTSIDE) instead of working INSIDE the business is not just pie-in-the-sky theoretical rhetoric. We know it works, if applied properly.

How do we know it works and how have we learned these principles?

First, we have to make a confession. To be honest with you, the first number of years we ran our accounting practice, we were in the same boat as most of our clients. Our business was doing okay, but it was not truly being run as a business.

Just like John, we were spending countless hours creating financial statements, meeting with clients, preparing individual tax returns, corporate tax returns, sales tax returns, payroll tax returns, bank reconciliations, and so on.

We were no different than your stereotypical CPA firm. We were working a zillion hours in tax season at the sacrifice of our family and personal lives.

We realized that there had to be a better way to make a living and to run a successful accounting business. We looked around us at all of the accountants we knew, and they all seemed to fall into three categories, none of which we wanted to follow. The owners/partners were either alcoholics, divorced, or dead from heart attacks, or a lovely combination of the three. We don't know about you, but none of those options appealed to us.

Because of that, we have spent the last 20-plus years transforming our business and putting into place the principle of running an accounting firm that does accounting, versus working inside an accounting firm that does accounting—and helping clients do the same in their businesses.

We have been there, done that. We are not going to tell you to do anything we have not done personally. We've made a ton of mistakes along the way and have learned from them and want to keep you from making the same mistakes that we have made.

While working with small business owners over the past 30 years, it became apparent to us that small business owners didn't have a clue on how to "work outside" and run a profitable small business.

We found ourselves time and time again working with clients, trying to teach them the principles of *running* a profitable small business instead of working *inside* that small business. When done properly, working outside their businesses resulted in a lot more profits than working inside their businesses would have—just as it has done for us.

We wanted nothing more than to pass that knowledge on to them so that they wouldn't have to make the same mistakes we made, and saw hundreds of clients make as well. This gave them the opportunity to reach their goals in a much faster time frame than we had.

We believe in the old adage: "Don't reinvent the wheel, Learn from others and learn from others mistakes."

This journey is not going to be easy. You have a lot to learn, and probably just as much, if not more, to unlearn.

Things are going to have to be different in and around your business if you want to increase your profits by building a successful small business the correct way.

The first thing you must understand is going to come as a surprise to most of you.

YOUR BUSINESS SHOULD NOT BE YOUR LIFE

Repeat that: YOUR BUSINESS SHOULD NOT BE YOUR LIFE.

You should not just create a job for yourself and then be a slave to your business.

The purpose of your business is to serve you and your family, not the other way around.

We all know that life is way too short to be a slave to your business.

You must work to live, not live to work.

Read the previous paragraphs and burn them into your memory.

The second thing you need to understand is that you need to stop working INSIDE your business. You need to stop thinking and believing that you are the "expert," even though you might be, and start being the "expert" at working OUTSIDE your business.

Here comes the bat again. You need to lose the ego, pal.

You heard us, and we don't want any lip about it. Lose the ego!

We guarantee you that this will be the hardest thing to do. We know—it was the hardest thing for us to do. We are the experts in tax, accounting, payroll, etc. We went to college, graduate school, etc. We are the CPAs. We have the Master's Degree in Taxation. No one can prepare a tax return as well as we can. No one can deal with clients and give them advice as well as we can, etc., etc., etc.

We don't care what business you are in, losing your ego will be difficult at best.

We know what you are thinking. "But Tony and Frank, but Tony and Frank, no one can do the job as well as I can. I'm the expert."

Blah, blah, blah, blah, blah, blah, blah...

Do you see the little tear in the corner of our eyes?

Start to become the expert in the right areas. Get your head out of your bottom side, and lose the ego. Period. End of story.

CHAPTER 4

ARE YOU WORKING HARDER FOR LESS MONEY?

Sooooo.....tell the truth. Are you working harder now than you ever have for less money?

It is no secret that small businesses owners work far more than they should for the profits they are getting.

Does that sound familiar to you? Is that a problem for any of you? Are you burning the candle at both ends? Are you totally stressed out? Do you want to quit the business and go to work for someone else? Are you tired of dealing with employees? Are you tired of dealing with customers or clients? Are you tired of dealing with suppliers? Are you tired of juggling all of the plates you need to on a daily basis?

It's pretty ironic because the only people who understand the previous paragraph are the ones who are in, or have been in, business for themselves.

If you ask anyone who has never been self-employed, that person wouldn't have a clue as to what you are talking about or feeling. We are sure you've heard it before: "You must be rich; you are in business for yourself. You can do what you want, when you want to. You don't have a boss to kiss up to. You're making money hand over fist ... "

We all know that this couldn't be farther from the truth.

Here is the true heart of the problem. It is not that you don't work hard or put in your time (well for some of you that might be the issue)... the problem is that you are putting your time in doing the WRONG work.

Did you hear us??? You are doing the WRONG work in your business and that needs to stop right now!

We will address this concept throughout the book and show you, the owner of the company, how to do the right work. We think a lot of you will be totally surprised by the revelations you will have as you read further.

Whether you believe this or not, to get a quick snap shot of how your business functions, all you have to do is look at your personal life. In most instances, your business will mirror your personal life. Let us give you a few examples.

If you have written goals, plans for the future, direction in your personal life, a vision and tenacity to stick with it, your business will be running the same way. If you are just living day to day with no goals, no plans for the future, saving when and if you can, your business will be the same.

Your business will most likely be extremely organized if your personal life is. On the flip side, if you are extremely disorganized personally, guess what? Your business will most probably be also.

Your business will be a disaster, if your home is a disaster. Your business will run efficiently and successfully, if your home does. Your business truly reflects who you are.

Did we strike a nerve?

This is a pretty hard pill to swallow. Once you swallow the pill and drink the Kool-Aid, there is only one conclusion you can come to:

For your life and your business to change and improve, you must have a completely different attitude about your business and yourself. You've certainly heard the following statement from Zig Ziglar: "Your attitude, not your aptitude, determines your altitude!"

You can't just keep sitting back like John, thinking that time will not catch up with you, because IT WILL!

You are going to have to change first.

We can't emphasize this enough. If you can't change, or are unwilling to change, your business and your life will never reach their full potential. If you are hard-headed like John, neither will you or your family ever reach your full potential and become part of the independently wealthy 2% club. You will be doomed to the 98% club with the rest of the wannabes.

You need to start working smarter, not harder.

How does working less and making more money sound to you?

That is what your goal needs to be, but you must be able and willing to change to make it happen.

You have heard us before, and you will hear it again. If you are not willing to change, then stop reading right now, put the book down, and give it to someone else who has the mindset to improve his or her business and life.

If you can make the commitment to change, want to work less, and make more, then keep reading.

CHAPTER 5

WHY DID YOU GO INTO BUSINESS?

Sooooo.....why did you go into business?

Have you ever asked yourself this question before? If you haven't, you need to ask yourself right now.

WE CAN'T HEAR YOU!!!

We said, ask yourself the question: Why did you go into business in the first place?

What's the matter? Don't you really want to know the answer?

You don't have to tell us why you went into business...we already know why. How do we know, you might ask? Well, let us tell you how we know. We know because many years ago, it was the same reason we went into business for ourselves and the same reason that almost every business owner goes into business for himself or herself.

We are going to tell you our story first. See if it sounds familiar to you. We'd be willing to bet it does.

Our story goes something like this: We are very good accountants. We are tired of working for "the man." We are tired of being told what to do and when to do it. We are tired of working all of the zillions of hours and having "the man" make all the money. We are tired of not being appreciated. We are tired of kissing the proverbial boss's butt. We are tired of the partners taking all of the profits of the job to make themselves look better, even though we did all of the work and made all of the profit (you accountants out there will understand that one!!).

Why are we working for this moron? Hell, we know as much, if not more, about accounting and taxes than he does. We have the Master Degree in Taxation; he barely graduated high school, and if he's lucky, has two brain cells working at the same time, and he has to stand up to give those brain cells some air. He's a moron (did I say that already?) If it weren't for us, he would be out of business.

Apparently any moron (there we go again) can run a business; he's doing it, isn't he? This will be a piece of cake. We can hang out our shingle and have more work than we know what to do with.

Does all of that sound familiar to you?

Do you know what that is called?

That is called the potential business owner's brain fart!

How many of you went through the same thing? We'd bet it is most the folks reading this book, because it doesn't matter what business you went into—the scenario is always the same.

We know another thing, also. Once the bug bit you, and you had the business owner's brain fart, you couldn't get rid of it, could you? You thought about it day and night, didn't you? It consumed you, didn't it?

Whether it was a good idea or a bad idea at the time, it didn't matter how much risk was involved, you were going to open your own business and nothing was going to stop you, or get in your way. Not your boss, not your family, not your pastor, not your priest, not your account-ant, not your friends, not your colleagues. And especially not the lack of money and capital.

NOTHING or NOBODY was going to stop you now.

The internal gases were building up and had to be expelled. Look out world—here comes the big, bad, wannabe business genius!

Here comes the bat again. The only problem with the business owner brain fart is that it makes you go into business for the WRONG reason.

You heard us. *You went into business for the wrong reason.* Period. End of story.

We know what you are thinking: "What did you say? For the wrong reason. No, that's impossible. You guys are nuts. I knew exactly what I was doing?"

Really?

You might have thought you were doing it for the right reason, but that still doesn't change the fact that if the above story hit home with you, then just like when we started our business, it was for the wrong reason.

Read on and learn the real reason you should have gone into business. It is going to surprise you.

CHAPTER 6

WHY *SHOULD* YOU HAVE GONE INTO BUSINESS?

Sooooo.....why *should* you have gone into business?

What should be the real purpose for going into any business?

We guarantee you will not guess the reason. It is probably the last reason you would have chosen. And, it doesn't matter what business you want to open; it could be any business in the world. Are you ready?

THE PURPOSE OF GOING INTO BUSINESS IS NOT TO CREATE A JOB FOR YOURSELF. THE PURPOSE OF GOING INTO BUSINESS IS TO CREATE JOBS FOR OTHER PEOPLE AND MAKE MONEY FROM THEIR EFFORTS SO THAT YOU CAN EVENTUALLY BECOME INDEPENTENLY WEALTHY.

That's it. It is as simple as that.

Repeat it again out loud! Did it sink in? If not, repeat it again, and again, until it does sink in. We know some of you are more stubborn and slower than others and need to repeat it for several hours, but stay with it until your brain fully absorbs this concept!!

You absolutely, without a doubt, must understand that concept. If you don't understand it and start to make it a reality, you will be doomed.

You cannot continue to be the Producer in your business. The Producer is the person who is mainly responsible for producing (duh!) the goods or services that your business provides.

In our case, at the accounting firm, the Producer is the one who meets with the clients, produces the clients' monthly financial statements, tax returns, sales tax returns, bank reconciliations, tax planning meetings, payrolls, does the sales, and so on and so on.

In your business, it might be the carpenter who builds houses, the attorney who writes contracts, the insurance agent who sells policies, the computer geek who fixes the computers, the barber who cuts the hair, the landscaper that cuts the grass... the list goes on.

Do you get it???

Here comes the bat again. By now you should have realized that we are not going to hold back in what we need to tell you.

We know this next statement is harsh and cruel, but it's the truth. Every one of you who is the Producer in his or her business must listen to this. If all that you want to be is the Producer and Producer only in your business, then....

GET A JOB WORKING FOR SOMEONE ELSE!

You heard us right. Get a job working for someone else. Close your doors today! If you're an accountant, come to the Chicago area, we'll hire you. We are always looking for good Producers.

There is no right or wrong about which path you are going to take. If you don't want to take any risks and are a Producer at heart, you are doing what you want to do, and that's what makes you happy, then by all means—be a Producer! But be a Producer for someone else and get out of your own business.

You don't need all of the day-to-day stress, hassles, headaches, and financial risks of running your own business.

Every great business owner needs plenty of great Producers working for him or her. In fact, the vast majority of Americans are Producers, and there is nothing wrong with that.

If you haven't figured it out by now, it takes a very special and distinct personality to be an owner of a business. However, if you have chosen the path of being an OWNER of a small business—you need to start acting like one!!

You are, as we see it, at a junction in the road. Which fork are you going to take, the left or the right? The choice, of course, is yours. If you go down the left path, it is basically the same path you've been on since you started your business. For whatever reason, whether you are hard-headed and *won't* change, don't know how to change (we can help you there), don't have the time or energy to change, or whatever excuse you can come up with, you are going to stay on that same business path.

It is on this left path, if you continue to stay on it, that most businesses will fold up and close their doors. Here is why:

You are burned out, or soon will be burned out. You are not making as much money as you thought. You are putting in way too many hours, not seeing your family, going deeper and deeper into debt just to make payroll and pay your bills. Again, the list goes on.

Stay on the left path and you will have nothing but more of the same, forever!

We have said it before, and will say it again. Get out of business if this is the path you are going to stay on.

The right path looks totally different and will require a totally different mindset. Remember the Wizard of Oz? Well, Dorothy, it is time to follow the right Yellow Brick Road path!

You are going to have to change the business and take it to the next level. You need to stop being the Producer in your business and start to steer your business in a different direction.

We like to use analogies and this is the perfect time for one. Basically, your business is like a boat on the ocean. Right now, the boat is floating on the ocean without a rudder and captain, and is at the mercy of the winds. The boat has plenty of crew to do the work ("producers"), but no captain to lead them. Your boat needs a leader and a captain. You have to be that person!!!

Did you hear us??? You have to steer the boat, you have to stop swabbing the decks, mate. You have to step up and be the captain—but first, you have to change the reason you went into business.

Remember: THE PURPOSE OF GOING INTO BUSINESS IS NOT TO CREATE A JOB FOR YOURSELF. THE PURPOSE OF GOING INTO BUSINESS IS TO CREATE JOBS FOR OTHER PEOPLE AND MAKE MONEY FROM THEIR EFFORTS SO THAT YOU CAN EVENTUALLY BECOME INDEPENTENLY WEALTHY.

You have to be the captain!! Start acting like one!

Write it down and memorize it. Put it under your pillow and absorb it through osmosis if you have to. You must understand this concept, Captain.

Do not read another page until you have burned that fact into your brain!!!

## CHAPTER 7

ARE YOU AND YOUR BUSINESS ONE?

Sooooo.....are you and your small business one? Let's take a look at a typical small business scenario.

This happened to us when we started our small business and we will bet it happened to you as well. In the typical business scenario, the small business owner, and the business itself, are ONE AND THE SAME.

You'll probably have to re-read that sentence for it to sink in. Go on, re-read it...don't be afraid!

Let us explain this sad truth....

If you were not working inside your business anymore, for whatever reason, the sad fact is that your small business would cease to exist.

Your business would cease to exist because you ARE the business, you are the Producer. Without you, your business absolutely, positively, could not, and would not, function or survive.

Are we right??? You bet we are.

For all of you Doubting Thomases out there who don't believe us, ask yourself a few questions. After that, we want you to honestly answer them and quit kidding yourself.

Can you take a two-month vacation without your business coming to a complete halt or suffering greatly? How about one month? How about one week? How about one day? If you got hit by a bus today and were laid up for a few months, or were sick and had to have surgery, would your business run smoothly without you? What if you had a massive heart attack and died; would your business survive you?

If you answered "no" to any one of the questions above, we have proven our point.

Your business and you are one. Without you, it would stop.

If you did answer "no," there is a lot of work, learning, and change in your business that needs to be done. Are you up for it?

If you answered "yes" to all of the questions above, congratulations are in order because you are on that yellow brick road!

Chapter 8

What's In A Name?

Sooooo.....what's in a small business name?

Choose your business name carefully!

Your business name will be with you for a long time and it is very difficult to change it down the road. Yes, it can be done. We did it, but believe us, it is much easier to get it right from the beginning than to change it later.

We wish someone would have slapped Tony upside his head years ago when he opened his business and named it "Anthony Fiore, CPA," which later was changed to "Accounting Freedom, Ltd." It would have saved a ton of grief, aggravation, and money.

Think about all the items that need to be changed when you change the name of your business: letterheads, envelopes, websites, invoicing, payables, advertising pieces, logo, brand, getting the word out to clients and customers so they don't think you went out of business, changing your sign, licensing, and so on and on.

If your name is established and needs to be changed, don't waste any time. Come up with an appropriate name and make the change now.

We can't give you suggestions on what the business name should be, but we can and will give you a suggestion on what the name of the business SHOULD NOT be.

The business should *never* be named after YOU! You heard us right. Never, never, ever, name the business after you, unless you are required by the laws of your state or licensing boards to do so.

We will explain why in the next chapter....

This is especially a problem and prevalent in most service industries. In most cases, owners name the small business after themselves. Here are some examples, and we know you can think of many more on your own.

When Tony started the accounting firm in 1981, it was originally named "Anthony Fiore, CPA." The mechanic around the corner named his business "Scott's Garage." The barber downtown named his business "Steve's Barber Shop." The local plumber named his business

"Sam's Plumbing." The landscaper named his business "Joe Smith, Landscaping." The shoe repairman named his business, "Frank's Shoe Repair."

Just think about it. Look around your town—you will see hundreds of examples of this mistake.

Why do we do this? Why do almost all business owners name their business after themselves?

We can tell you the many reasons why Tony did it and we will bet this will hit home with most of you also.

It was an ego thing.

- I'm a CPA *(Big deal)*.
- I've earned the degree *(Another big deal)*.
- I'm a cut above *(In your mind only, pal)*.
- I like to see my name on the door *(Get some better glasses)*.
- Everyone else in the industry does it *(So let's be a follower)*.
- The clients and employees need to know who the boss is! *(Get over yourself, would you?)*
- It was easy and I couldn't think of anything else *(Great imagination)*.
- No one told me it was the wrong thing to do *(Probably the only limited excuse that has merit)*.

It's time to LOSE the ego, and get a little smarter!!!

CHAPTER 9

WHY IS NAMING THE BUSINESS AFTER ME A MISTAKE?

Sooooo.....why is naming a small business after the owner a mistake? It is not just a mistake—it is a HUGE mistake.

By naming the small business after you, you are insuring that the business and you will be one and the same, forever!

Think about what relationship you have created with your clients/customers by doing this up to this point. The clients/customers completely depend on YOU, YOUR knowledge, YOUR expertise, YOUR talent, etc.

The clients are buying YOUR ability to give them what they want, NOT YOUR BUSINESS's ability to give them what they want.

Repeat this. It is totally critical to you to understand this point. *They want you, not your business.*

They are looking for the main man or woman whose name is on the door to help them. In their mind, they don't want to deal with any flunky employee, no matter how competent they are.

They want the owner, period, end of story, and will settle for nothing less.

Do not make the same mistake that we made. Originally, our clients were always looking for Tony to help them with their taxes, their financial statements, their tax and business planning, and so on. At first, it was very rewarding and really stroked the ego. Tony was helping clients, making money, and feeling great about himself and what he had accomplished.

Clients were coming in to see the main MAN!!!

But we guarantee you, it was the WRONG way to build a business and will take years to correct. Believe us, we know. It took years to undo that mistake in our accounting practice. Finally, after all of those years of undoing the mistake, clients are now coming into Accounting Freedom, Ltd. because of what Accounting Freedom, Ltd. can provide for them—and not because of what Tony or Frank can help them with.

Someday, Tony, Frank, and everyone else who works here will be gone, but the business will survive and be able to service clients for many, many years into the future.

You see, it is not only about you and your family. By building a business that will survive, you are providing a safety net for you, your family, your employees and their families, and most importantly, the clients or customers who depend on you.

Ask yourself some other questions. We have already talked about the vacation part, but what about these?

What if you wanted to be somewhere else, for example, at home eating bonbons, coaching, or watching your kids' sports team, at the mall (shopping, ugh...), or other activities you might find pleasurable?

What if you were sick, or just wanted to play hooky and didn't want to go into your business for a couple of days.

What if, at the spur of the moment, an opportunity came up to take the trip of your dreams—could you do that right now?

If the business completely depends on you for every-thing, you don't truly own a business, you have and own a job. ***Did you get that?***

We have told you this before and we are going to keep pounding it into your brain until your eyes bleed.

All you have done is created a job for yourself. All you have done is created a job for yourself. All you have done is created a job for yourself. All you have done is created a job for yourself. All you have done is created a job for yourself. All you have done is created a job for yourself. All you have done is created a job for yourself.

Did you get it yet?

What's worse, you are probably working for much more of a maniac than you did in your previous real job and that maniac is YOU!

If you are opening a small business, name it correctly. If you currently own a small business, and it is named after you, change the name, now!

This is the first step to recovery.

You must start to get clients or customers coming to your business for what your business can provide them, NOT for what you can personally provide to them.

You are going to have to do this one way or another if your business is successful. The more successful it becomes, the more you can't rely on just yourself.

You will not be able to do everything all alone.

At this point in time, if you don't change, we guarantee you that your small business will start to collapse and implode.

Why will your small business start to collapse and implode, you might ask?

Because we said it will.

We've seen it before with many of our clients, and we have personally experienced it. Read on and we will explain why.

CHAPTER 10

WHY WILL MY BUSINESS COLLAPSE AND IMPLODE?

Sooooo.....why will my small business collapse and implode?

We are going to give you a scenario that we think will hit home with you if your business has been successful.

If everything goes well, your business begins to grow, clients and customers are returning. They are referring their family and friends. Your reputation in your town is growing. You've become involved in the Chamber of Commerce and other organizations. The cash in your bank account is increasing.

At first, it's great to see your business grow. You are making more money and getting more work and making more money.

Man, this is what it is all about! This is why I left my job and started my own business. I'm my own boss. I only have to answer to me. Look out, world! Here I come!!

But, we can assure you, as sure as the sun will come up tomorrow, something will begin to change because it always does. It has to if you are successful and your business is growing.

It is completely logical but unavoidable. Think about it for a second. As the business grows, so will the demands on your time. It doesn't take a brain surgeon to figure that one out, pal.

Guess what?? As the demand on your time grows, there aren't going to be enough hours in the day to handle all of the "Producer" work that needs to be done in the business, AND all of the other jobs that a small business owner has to do.

Think about it and be honest with yourself for a change. We all know that in the beginning, you need to work long hours to get things established. That is a fact no one can argue with.

However, as the business grows, you are put into a catch 22 situation. How is it possible that you are going to be able to do all of the production to deliver the product or service, open the doors, sweep the floors, clean the bathrooms, wait on or meet with the clients/customers, do all of the ordering, answer the phones, send out invoices, pay your bills, do the estimating, throw out the trash, do the accounting, do the payroll, deal with customer/client support and issues? Did we say clean the bathrooms?

Do you know what this reminds us of?

Do you remember when you were a kid and went to the circus or watched *Bozo's Circus* on TV (that sure dates Tony, doesn't it!!). Do you remember the performer who spun the plates on top of a bunch of poles? Do you remember how they kept adding plates, one after another? Spin, spin, spin, add, add, and add.

So what is the normal result? You know because it is happening to you. You can only add a certain number of plates before they start to fall.

In the beginning, you can keep adding and handling the plates with no problem. But guess what, eventually you will start to drop each plate. One by one, each area (plate) starts to fall, little by little, then faster and faster.

There is no way possible that you can continue to spin all of them, or keep adding to them, and get everything done and done correctly. Superman himself couldn't handle all of this. If you don't do something soon, the entire stack will come crashing down.

So what is your normal reaction?

We know what you will do, because we did it also. You are going to work more hours. That 8-hour day becomes ten, doesn't it?

But guess what? The 10-hour day, after a while, won't cut it either. It turns into a 13- or 14-hour day, doesn't it? Then, that won't be enough either, so you add a couple of more hours after that, and a couple of more after that, then Saturdays, then Sundays.

The stress is mounting, isn't it?

Soon you will find that there just isn't enough time in the day to get it all done and to keep the plates spinning fast enough so that they don't fall.

Yeah, you can work 20-hour days for a while, but how long will that last before you burn out, get divorced, become an addict, or drop dead of a heart attack?

No matter how many hours you put in, we guarantee you, the more successful your business becomes, the plates will begin to fall, one by one, they will come crashing down!!

There is another bad side to this also.

Because time is limited and you have to squeeze it all in, we know another thing that is going to happen.

The jobs you are doing will become sloppier and will be done later and later. Clients/customers will start to complain.

We're right, aren't we?

The clients/customers start to ask themselves, "What happened to them? Their quality and service used to be top notch. We loved what they produced and now it is starting to suck."

You will also notice that the referrals you used to get from your loyal clients or customers are slowing down or have come to a grinding halt because you are not doing the great job you did before.

It takes days to call a potential client or customer back instead of minutes or hours. In fact, you are at the point where you don't even want to call them back because you know it is only going to add to your work load and problems, so you put it off.

You are going from one job to another and not finishing any one of them in the timely manner you once did.

You are spreading yourself too thin, aren't you? Be honest with yourself. It hurts, doesn't it?

Let's face it. If your business does grow and continues to grow, it is only logical: you can't do it all yourself. It is physically impossible! There is only one outcome possible if you keep on the same path you are on.

At this point, you want to run and hide don't you? You wish you hadn't opened this blasted business and that you stayed working for someone else. You are thinking to yourself, "Let them worry about all of this nonsense. Just give me my paycheck so that I can go home and watch a ball game and drink some beer. 9 to 5 is looking pretty good right now."

What is happening to you has happened to thousands of business owners before you.

Your business is starting to collapse and implode!!

You have to get help or get out of business. You decide that you want to stay in business, so your only choice is to hire an employee or two.

You have to get organized. Keep reading and let's look at the first step to turning this ship around.

CHAPTER 11

WHAT'S THE FIRST STEP TO GETTING ORGANIZED?

S ooooo.....what's the first step to getting organized?

We are glad you asked. The first step you have to do is to create an Organizational Chart, like the one below:

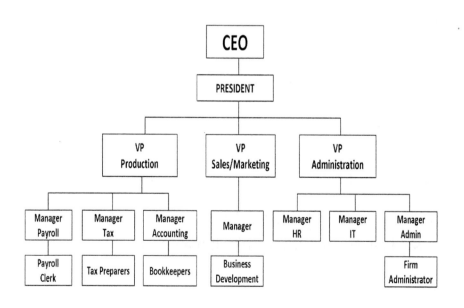

You might be saying to yourself right now, "Are these guys insane? What do I have to do that for? It's just a waste of time."

You couldn't be more dead wrong on this one. This is where you must start. Trust us, we know what we are talking about.

Get out your computer and draw it, or take out an old-fashioned pad of paper or a napkin you've been crying on and get to it.

Start now. Quit whining like a little baby, and draw an organizational chart of your business.

Sketch out all the boxes (job positions) that make your company work. For example, in our company (your company will have to be customized to your own boxes), the CEO is at the top, then underneath is the VP of the Accounting Department, VP of the Marketing, VP of the Tax Individuals, VP of the Tax Corporate, VP of the Payroll Department, and so on.

Under those boxes are the boxes of job positions to accomplish the work in each department: Managers, Bookkeepers, Tax Preparers, and others.

Continue down the chart until you finish drawing all of the boxes with the job titles in them.

Now, flip it end over end. Yes, that's correct. Flip it end over end. This is the way we should look at an organizational chart.

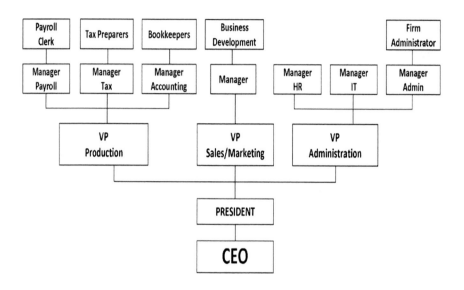

The CEO should be on the bottom acting in a supporting role, the trunk of the tree, supporting all of the branches of all the people above him/her. The CEO should not be on the top barking orders downward.

Now, fill in the boxes with the names of everyone who is responsible for each job activity.

This is where the fun begins because after you fill in all of the names, YOU ARE GOING TO WANT TO PUKE!!!

That's right, you're feeling sick to your stomach aren't you?

We know what is on the page, without your even telling us. Your name is in almost all of the boxes, isn't it?

Guess where your name should be?

It should only be in the CEO box! That's right, only in the CEO box at the bottom.

We know you are thinking to yourself right now, "Holy crap, we sure have a lot of work to do here. Is this even possible?"

Well, what are you waiting for?

Move to the next chapter for the next step to getting organized. Then let's start to really dig in.

CHAPTER 12

WHAT'S THE NEXT STEP TO GETTING ORGANIZED?

Sooooo.....what's the next step to getting organized?

Now that you have your Organization Chart completed and you've barfed your lunch, you need to start correcting this huge disaster.

Every box that has your name in it needs to be replaced with trained, competent, producing employees. That's right. Every box!

We know what you are thinking. "I can't afford to hire anyone. There isn't enough money. I have to do it myself."

Well, you couldn't be more dead wrong on all of those thoughts. You can't afford NOT to hire. Find the money somewhere. In the long run, if you hire and train your employees properly, your business will be a lot more profitable, you will have a lot more money, and you will be a lot saner.

However, this is not an easy process and could take a number of years to accomplish, but you need to start NOW. If you wait another year, it will take a year longer to accomplish your goal.

Start at the top (remember you have flipped the chart end over end) and work your way down the chart.

You must first work the boxes yourself. You are doing all of these jobs now, so this should be easy for you. You must, while working in those boxes, develop detailed job descriptions (what the job entails) for each box, along with a procedure manual (how to do the tasks) for that position. After those two things are accomplished, you must surround both of them with systems.

To put it another way: "How to do that job for dummies."

Anyone who simply knows how to read and has one brain cell working should be able to pick up the manual, read it, follow the system, and then be able to perform the task and complete the job.

Let us give you an example of what we mean.

Years ago, Tony used to do the payroll for his accounting firm. On one particular Friday morning, he did the payroll and then headed off to a seminar. One step in doing the payroll was to set up the payroll tax deposit that needed to be sent into the government that day to avoid any penalties. Yeah, you guessed it. He screwed up and hadn't set up the deposit. By the time he came back to the office in the late afternoon, he realized his mistake. However, the person who was trained and normally electronically sent the tax deposits in to the government was gone for the day.

Tony was on his own because he had never done this task before.

This could have been and should have been a "panic moment" for Tony. You know what we're talking about. It's the kind of moment when you realize you've done something pretty stupid. You feel sick to your stomach over it, can't believe you made such a dumb mistake, and you're at the point of filling your shorts. Yeah, you've been there before, haven't you?

Well, no need to worry. After a few seconds of "panic attack," Tony realized that it all would be okay, because … you guessed it! There was a procedure manual on how to submit the tax deposit.

Tony went to the procedure manual for payroll, flipped to the page for making the payroll tax deposits, followed the procedure, and was able to perform the task, even though he had never done it before.

Yeah, that's right, even a dummy like Tony could perform the task because his one brain cell was working that day and he simply knew how to read.

Do you understand the concept? Create procedures and systems for dummies!!!

You need to write down all these procedures. They shouldn't be just in your head and your head alone, or worse yet, in the head of an employee who will (in time) eventually leave.

Only when the procedure manual is written (this could be in outline form at first, and filled in with details as required) and the system is in place, should you hire someone.

You can even hire someone with no experience in the area so that you can train that person in your way of doing things.

Hire someone who is eager to learn how to do it right. Someone who is willing to learn what you have spent so much time and energy to develop and write down. Someone who is willing to WORK THE SYSTEM you have created.

Once that person is hired and trained, you can move on to the next box and start the process all over again.

As all of the boxes are filled, and your name is starting to be replaced with competent, trained people, you will be freed up to do more and more of the strategic work and planning that needs to be done.

As you can imagine, this process could take a while, but it needs to be done with each and every area.

WARNING!!

Hiring someone is difficult at best. Do not be discouraged in the hiring process and do not settle. Keep looking until you find the right person for the job, even if it takes a while.

We have made the mistake in our firm, numerous times, of being quick to hire and slow to fire. If the person is not working out, and is not the right person for the job, FIRE that person, sooner rather than later, and find someone who is right for the job.

Believe us, it is a hard thing to do, but you will be thankful that you did. A bad hire is like a cancer to your business—it will slowly destroy it from within.

As your good employees work the areas, get feedback from them on how to improve the manual, the procedures, and the systems in the areas for which they are responsible.

You have to be careful here and re-read the last paragraph. We said, get "feedback" from them. After you get the feedback, you must decide whether or not to change the manual, procedure, or system.

You do not change any of it because someone wants to do the task a different way.

You will only change the manual, procedure, or system if you can be shown it is a better and more efficient way to do the task, not just a different way.

Believe us. Employees will try to make you change just because they are used to doing it a different way and feel more comfortable with it.

But remember, YOU are the owner, the one in charge, the one steering the boat, and the one signing their pay checks. You are the one taking all of the risk, not your employees. So, don't be sucked into their nonsense. Got it? Change the manual, procedure, or system only if it is a better and more efficient way.

Now we want you to take a deep breath and slow down a little bit, here because we would be willing to bet that you don't realize something else.

We'll bet you don't have a clue about setting up a system. Let's take a look at how to do just that in the next chapter.

CHAPTER 13

WHAT'S YOUR SYSTEM?

Sooooo.....what's your system?

You must set up systems for all aspects of your business. They will be the blueprint for how all of your employees are to perform their jobs.

Setting up systems is one of the most important tasks you will have to do in your business. The systems you create will run the business; the people you hire must run and follow those systems.

You must repeat the last sentence and burn it into your brain. *The systems you create will run the business; the people you hire must run and follow those systems.*

You must write down "how to do" procedures for every task and every job that needs to be done, or is done, in your business on a daily basis.

And we mean EVERYTHING!!

The system needs to say to everyone: "This is how we do IT here." The "IT" in the last sentence truly refers to everything that is done at your business.

Let us give you a few examples to bring the point home. The first example you might consider minor to the second example, which demonstrates a more substantial procedure. Minor or major, all systems need to be thought through and written down.

Let us ask you a few simple questions to demonstrate a minor example. How do you answer the phone at your business? Is it the same way every time? If you have employees, do they answer it the same way every time? Do they answer it the same way you do?

We would bet the answer is "No, we don't answer it the same way." Everyone in the business must answer the phone the same way. You must write out the procedure of "How to answer the phone." This might sound stupid and silly to you, but it is at the heart of what we are talking about.

The systems you create will run the business; the people you hire must run and follow those systems.

Remember???

In our office, everyone, and we mean everyone, answers the phone the same way based upon a written procedure that we wrote a number of years ago. When our phone rings you will hear.... "Good Morning (afternoon), Accounting Freedom and Payroll Specialists. This is (name). How may I help you?"

Now, let's look at a more major example from our office. We have written a procedure on how to process a tax return. Unlike the phone procedure above, which is one tiny paragraph, the tax return procedure is multiple pages long.

It explains in detail every aspect of handling a tax return, from the moment a client calls for an appointment, or drops off a tax return, to the moment a client picks it up, and everything in between.

You can imagine the detail that needs to be in that sucker, and we mean detail. Nothing is left to chance. Nothing is left to the discretion of the staff, from the receptionist (when the call or return comes in), to the clerical staff, the tax preparer, the manager for review, back to the receptionist (for pickup or delivery).

Everything is written out and nothing is left (or as little as possible) to the discretion of the employees.

As you can imagine, it took a long, long time to write it and perfect it, but anyone with one brain cell can read it and perform the tasks.

Do you get it now???

Everything needs to be written down as to how YOU want it done at your business, and then you need to make sure it is followed through, with NO exceptions.

You want the business to run like a well-oiled machine, with all of the parts running together and smoothly. This system, this machine, you have created, must be designed to consistently satisfy your clients or customers every single time they do business with you.

As the owner, this is what you should be concerned about and what you should be focusing your time on.

The system isn't something you just make up out of thin air. It is something you create from building and working inside your business over the years.

Let's face it. Who knows better than you how to best perform a task in your business. As the Producer, you've been doing it for how many years already?

Write it down, and make sure everyone else does it your way. Everything needs to be standardized. If you design the system properly, thinking through every possible problem and solution, then all any employee has to do is learn how to follow and run the system.

Let's come at this from a different perspective if you don't quite get it yet.

You need to "Franchise It."

Let's take a look at what that means.

CHAPTER 14

FRANCHISE IT?

S ooooo.....what does "Franchise It" mean?

In simple terms, you must franchise the business.

Well, we know what you are asking now: "What the heck does that mean??"

Let's take a deeper look....

But first you must do some initial pretending. You need to put on your little play hat. Let's pretend that the business you own IS going to be the model of the business empire that you want to create.

Let's pretend that your dream is to open many additional businesses in the future, EXACTLY LIKE the business you are running now. It doesn't matter if you are never going to open up another location, open only one more, or open 100,000 more—the thought process is the same.

The key phrase in the last paragraph is "EXACTLY LIKE." The other businesses need to be an exact carbon copy (carbon copy....is Tony dating himself again!!) and duplicate of the first business. Not ALMOST LIKE IT, BUT EXACTLY LIKE IT. An identical twin.

This is much easier said than done, as we discussed in the last chapter. Think about the extent of this project. Every aspect of the business must be written down in a Procedural Manual. From the moment your doors open in the morning until well after they close at night.

You also have to set up systems so that the business can be operated by the people with the lowest possible skill level necessary to complete their job in every location.

For example, in our accounting business, we need accountants and bookkeepers, but we don't have to hire brilliant people with expert knowledge and a zillion years of experience.

We must create the very best system through which good accountants and good bookkeepers can be hired and be able to produce consistent, exceptional results for our clients.

In fact, when we hire a bookkeeper in our business, we always look for people who have the skills to BECOME a great bookkeeper, not for a person who HAS the skills already.

We usually shy away from people who have multiple years of bookkeeping experience because we want to train them on our system. If they have experience, they will have to first unlearn their old habits and then learn our system.

The question we need to keep asking ourselves is:

"How can we give our clients or customers what they want through a reliable, reproducible system, rather than relying on employees to produce these results based upon how they see fit from their previous work experience or knowledge?

In other words: How can we create a business whose end result (producing a consistent product and creating loyal clients/customers) is dependent on the SYSTEMS we've painstakingly created, rather than on the PEOPLE we have hired and the knowledge, experience, or expertise they bring with them?

How can we create an expert system rather than looking to hire experts?

Don't get us wrong here. We are not saying that the quality of the people you hire is not important. It's just the opposite. The quality of the people you hire is very important to the success of the systems you've created.

The systems you've set up will give them exactly what they need to succeed and blossom if they are loyal, honest, and have good work ethics.

The best businesses out there are not built by hiring expert employees. They are truly built by everyday, ordinary people who are able to accomplish extraordinary things because of who they are personally, and because of the systems that the owners have put into place in their businesses.

You must spend the time, think through, and set up each system in your business. This step is essential to the success of your businesses.

Think about it for a second. Everyone you hire will have different levels of knowledge, different skills, prior training, prior experiences, and so on.

The only way to get everyone on the same page is to have systems in place. The system, when followed, will ensure that your employees are well trained and can do their jobs incredibly well, each and every time.

The system will also allow you to train and get each employee up to speed and running faster.

Take a look around you at any of the extremely successful businesses in the world with which we are all familiar: McDonald's, Starbucks, Kentucky Fried Chicken, Microsoft, Walgreens—the list goes on. Whether you have figured it out already or not, they are all successful because of their systems.

You could go into any McDonald's in the world and the burgers and fries are all made the same way, with the same ingredients, with the same equipment. Any Starbucks and the specific coffee that you order (some names we can't even pronounce), will be made the same, from location to location, no matter what part of the world you are in.

If a McDonald's employee is making a hamburger, it is not up to his discretion as to what meat to use, what bun, what condiments to use, or how long to cook it. ALL of that has already been determined. The system to make the hamburger, fries, shakes, coffee, or whatever, has been predetermined and is written down in procedure manuals to help in training the new employees.

They MUST follow the system that is developed and already in place, with NO exceptions. They must all use the same ingredients from the same suppliers. Everything in those businesses have been standardized and predetermined in advance. That is the key to their success and growth.

Look around you now that you are aware of this fact. You will notice system-based businesses and be able to differentiate them from other businesses that are people-driven, rather than systems-driven.

However, to have well-oiled, successful systems, you absolutely need to hire the right employees and each employee must be in the right seat on the bus in your business.

We'll bet you don't realize that there is a wrong way and a right way to hire any employee.

You have to make sure you do it right, because doing it wrong could cost you dearly.

Keep reading. Let's examine how NOT to do it.

CHAPTER 15

WHAT'S THE WRONG WAY
TO HIRE?

Sooooo.....what's the wrong way to hire an employee?

We hope by this point you have finally realized that in order to run the business successfully, you are going to need to set up systems and then hire some help.

Well, it's about time that you woke up!

Let's recap: You've developed the organizational chart, you've developed the job description, you've written, or started writing, the procedure manual for that job, and you have started developing the systems for your business.

Well, have you? If you haven't, don't read any further. Yeah, that's right. Put down this book, and get to work developing the necessary tools to make yours a hiring success story instead of a hiring disaster story.

Without them, you possibly could be successful in your hiring process, but it will probably be more based upon sheer luck.

Once you have those tasks completed, come back and continue reading.

Soooo, you've got it all done?

It's a great start to learning how to run a business. You have quantified what job needs to be done, what the job entails, and how to do the job. Now all you have to do is find the right person.

Now, now. Slow down a bit. Don't just rush to Craig's List and post an ad in the local newspaper, or hire your sister-in-law.

Did you know that there is a wrong way and a right way to hire an employee?

Before you jump off the cliff and make another HUGE mistake, let's examine the wrong way to hire.

Unfortunately, the wrong way to hire is normally the path most business owners take because of lack of knowledge on how to hire and because it normally is the easy way out.

Let us tell you about our first hires many years ago. If you have ever hired anyone, your story is probably the same.

We finally decided to hire a bookkeeper. Let's say her name is Sally. We went through the hiring process, (which we knew nothing about), and we think we've gotten lucky. The person we've hired has five years of experience in bookkeeping and seems like our perfect solution. On her first day, we gave her a quick talk and tour, show her the ropes for five minutes, and turn her loose. She takes to it like a fish to water. Once in a while, she asks some minor questions, but not a lot, and does her work day in and day out.

Things seem great, as time went on, we gave Sally more and more responsibilities. We could finally start to cut back our hours from 16 to 12 a day. We can actually take a lunch once in a while. This is really cool! Why didn't we do this a long time ago?

The business continued to grow and expand. Sally was starting to get swamped and was going to need help. We told her to hire the people she needed. Sally hired and trained them. Everything seemed to be going great. Sally was a gift from Heaven. How in the world had we done it without her?

The business continued to grow and expand.

However, things start to slowly fall apart and we saw the plates starting to fall again....

A client called us to complain about his financial statements being late and that the numbers were all wrong. We try to calm the client down and tell him that we would talk to Sally to find out why and get back to them.

Another client called and complained that she felt like she was being treated like a second-hand client and not getting the attention she once received and deserved. "It's not like when you were taking care of us personally." She decided to switch accountants.

We looked at a client's bank reconciliation that John (whom Sally had hired) worked on, and exploded. "What kind of garbage work is this? Where did you learn how to do it this way? A fifth grader could have done a better job. Give it to me! I'll do it. It needs to be correct and it needs to get done right now. The client needs it today."

The next day, we reviewed a tax return completed by Sue (whom Sally had hired). We couldn't believe our eyes! We think to ourselves, "A six-year-old kid could have done a better job than this." So we fix it ourselves before it goes to the client.

This is only the beginning of when the plates began to fall faster and faster than when we were doing everything for ourselves.

From the land of hard knocks, we believed we had just learned an important real world fact. We should never have hired and trusted Sally to get the job done. We never should have trusted Sally to hire the other employees. We shouldn't have trusted anyone but ourselves. We are idiots. Why didn't we know this was going to happen. Why hadn't we seen this coming?

We realized that no employee was going to replace us as owners because none of them care as much as we do. They are all lazy and don't have the knowledge to do it right. Did we say they don't care?

A light bulb went off in our heads and we came to the realization that if the job was going to get done right, we would have to bite the bullet and just do it ourselves.

So we started to do some of the jobs again—bank reconciliations, tax returns, financial statements, and client meetings. And guess what happened? The more we did, the less our employees did. A lovely inverse relationship had started.

We asked ourselves, "What were we doing this for? It was so much better when we were on our own, when we were smaller. We are going to fire everyone and down-size!"

Does this scenario sound familiar??? What a ridiculous way to run a business and to hire employees.

So let's get going. Learn the right way to hire. There is a better way that will work for you.

Hold on to your hat. It's not what you think!

CHAPTER 16

WHAT'S THE RIGHT WAY TO HIRE?

Sooooo.....what's the right way to hire an employee?

This is the age-old question that we struggled with for many, many years because we were doing it all wrong.

Let's take a look at the typical path we followed. We're sure it will ring true with you as well.

We needed to hire a bookkeeper, sooooo what did we do? We placed an ad in the paper for someone who had experience in bookkeeping and hired according to how many years of experience the person had......WRONG!!!

What a dumb way to do it, even though it is the typical, conventional way, right?

You need someone to work for you so you look for someone with experience in that area, or worse yet, you are impatient and hire anyone who can fog a mirror. We believe that is a crucial mistake.

Have you done all of the things you were supposed to do in the preceding chapters? Have you developed an organization chart, set up your systems, and then franchised your business?

If you haven't done those things, get back there and do them NOW! Do not, and we repeat, *do not,* hire anyone unless you have made a major dent in the preceding action items.

Your charts and procedures don't have to be totally complete or perfect, because they never will be. You will always be changing and tweaking the systems as your business develops.

Sooooo, quit using perfection as an excuse!

The best way that we have found to hire is to hire people based upon their personality, work ethic, honesty, patience, and loyalty. Yep, you heard me right. Hire base on personality, work ethic, honesty, patience, and loyalty—not on experience.

Think about it for a moment and you'll see that we are right. Let us explain further with an example.

Let's go back to our bookkeeper example. Today, we always look to hire a bookkeeper with NO bookkeeping experience. Someone with a great personality and work ethic, someone who is honest and loyal, someone who has an aptitude for math, and someone who is quick in processing and solving problems. If the person has all those traits, we can teach the person how to do book-keeping easily—if the new hire simply follows OUR system.

Think about what happens if the person has prior experience. First, he or she would have to unlearn most of what the person already knows and the bad habits from a previous job, before he or she would be effective and open-minded to following OUR system.

We have always had challenges with bookkeepers who have experience because they always want to do it their way and not ours.

Now, don't get us wrong. We are always looking for better and faster ways to do the tasks. If an employee can show us that he or she has a better, faster, and more efficient way of doing a task, we would by all means change our system to implement the improvements.

The key words are *better, faster, and more efficient.*

We will never change our tried and true system for employees who want to do a task differently because that was the way they learned it in their previous life.

The other part of hiring someone is personality, work ethic, honesty, and loyalty.

We don't care what system you have or don't have. You cannot teach anyone personality, work ethic, honesty, patience, or how to be loyal to you, your company, and your clients/customers. They either have it or they don't, period.

No amount of training or talking to that employee will ever be able to instill those traits. If you think you can, you have a sad road ahead of you. Believe us, we know. We have tried numerous times in the past and have failed miserably every single time.

You can't teach employees to be genuinely concerned about your clients or customers and to treat them as they would want to be treated.

You can't teach employees to not be jerks to everyone around them.

You can't teach employees to be loyal to you and the company.

You can't teach employees to be honest or patient.

You can't teach employees to have a passion for their work and to do their best at the job, day in and day out.

You can't teach employees to smile and be pleasant to clients, customers, or their other co-workers.

You can't teach employees to say, "I'm fine, thanks. How are you?" when someone asks the employee how he or she is doing, instead of just answering with, "Fine."

You can't teach employees not to be lazy when they are doing only what it takes to get by, and stay just under the radar.

You can't teach employees to go the extra mile for your business or your clients or customers.

Perhaps you have hired employees who were always trying to scam the system and were always looking out for number one, instead of looking out for the company, their co-workers, and the clients/customers?

They either have the burning desire to be successful at what they do and to go the extra mile for your business and its clients/customers, or they don't. Period.

I think you get the picture. You can teach them how to do a task and their job in your system, but you can't teach them personality, work ethic, honesty, patience. or loyalty.

You must also develop and have as a part of your system a way to get the most out of your employees.

## CHAPTER 17

HOW TO GET THE MOST OUT OF YOUR EMPLOYEES?

Sooooo.....how do you get the most out of your employees?

Let's take one step back first because we think there is another thing worth mentioning.

Just a friendly word of advice here: If you find a great employee who has the personality traits you are looking for and he or she is working your system properly and efficiently, do whatever it takes to keep that diamond in the rough with the company. Great employees are hard to find. Treat such gems fairly, with respect, and how you would want to be treated and they will be loyal to you and the company for many years.

Now, back to getting the most out of your employees.

There is a basic principle you need to follow in order to get the most out of your employees: ***You must set up a system to monitor their activity.***

In setting up this system, you only need to keep four little words in mind, but you need to learn them and burn them into your memory. We had it burned into our brains by a colleague of ours named David Compton at a conference we attended. We are forever grateful to him because it definitely changed our entire thought process of monitoring employees.

The four little words: "*Expect what you inspect.*"

Read it again, and burn it into your brain. It is such a simple concept but it is very, very, profound.

Expect what you inspect.

Let's look a little deeper. Your system has to have checks and balances in it. You need to set up a system so that you can easily inspect what each employee is doing.

Don't take this wrong. We are not suggesting this from a negative standpoint. We are not suggesting this because you need to spy on your employees to make sure they are doing their job.

If you hire the right employees, you will not and should not do anything like that. The monitoring we are talking about is to help improve the employee's performance, ability, production, and profitability.

However, if you or your department heads are not inspecting the production and the output on a systematic regular basis, you probably will just get garbage.

Your system needs to make sure that all employees are following the procedures and systems you have set up. The only way to do that is to "inspect" the output, so that you can "expect" the results you and your clients/customers need, want, and "expect" from your employees and your business.

Got it? *Expect what you inspect.*

Another phrase we have learned over the years also rings completely true. You need to burn this into your memory as well.

"If you don't measure it, you can't manage it."

Re-read this sentence again, and again, and again.....

"If you don't measure it, you can't manage it."

The monitoring systems you set up must accomplish this task also. You have to set up systems to monitor what is happening in all phases of your business.

Let me give you an extreme example of what happened to our accounting firm.

Years ago, the phrase "if you don't measure it, you can't manage it" finally got burned into our one brain cell, and caused us to really look at how we were monitoring our office. We came to the realization that we were monitoring to a certain small degree, but were very far from where we needed to be.

We were trying to monitor employees and production on multiple spreadsheets. Although this worked to a certain degree, it was very time consuming and inefficient to maintain and manage. We looked high and low for a software program that could monitor the production at an accounting firm. Guess what? There was nothing on the market that could do what we needed and wanted for our firm.

We made an extreme decision at that moment. We decided to write our own internal program. We started to do it internally at first and then we hooked up with a life-long friend who was a programmer and started really developing the software.

It was one of the best business decisions we have made. Today the software is used extensively in our firm. With the click of a mouse, we can "measure and manage" every aspect of our production.

In fact, we even started another company. We are selling the software to other accounting firms to help them monitor their production as well. A problem became an opportunity.

The moral: You must do whatever it takes to set up a system to monitor the day-to-day operations of your business. By measuring it, you and your employees will be able to manage it efficiently and effectively.

All of this will result in an increase in the profitability of your business.

Speaking of monitoring—what are the other keys to success???

## CHAPTER 18

WHAT ARE THE OTHER KEYS TO SUCCESS? PART 1

Soooo.....what are the other keys to success? Here's Part I.

What else should be looked at and analyzed regularly by a business owner?

The answer is simple, but often not done.....

The answer is your Financial Statements.

Being in the accounting business and dealing with small business owners for over 30 years, we can emphatically tell you that one of the worst mistakes a business owner can make is not to have regular, timely, and accurate financial statement numbers.

If you are a smaller business and don't have a CPA on staff, you must have a CPA firm do your financial statements on a regular, MONTHLY basis. You heard us right: *on a timely, regular, monthly basis.*

If your CPA firm has not suggested that, or if it tells you to do it yourself and bring it to them, either quarterly or annually, GET A NEW CPA FIRM—because that firm is not looking out for your best interests!!!!

Find a CPA firm that specializes in small- to medium-sized businesses and wants to work with you on an ongoing, regular, monthly basis—not just once per year at tax time.

We are not telling you this because we are in the accounting business. We are telling you this because we want you to be successful and profitable.

You're probably thinking, "But Tony and Frank, you don't understand. We can't afford to pay a CPA firm to do the financials and payroll."

We say, "Hogwash."

Keeping track of your financials is one cost you should never, ever, try to skimp on. We have seen it, time and time again, and we guarantee, it will come back to bite you where the sun doesn't shine in the future.

You must build this expense into your budget. It is a necessary expense like your utilities, rent, material costs, and other operating costs. Those expenses are built into your budget because you MUST pay them. This expense is no different. Put it into your budget, period!

Working with a great CPA firm is a tremendous asset and the cornerstone of the financial side of your business. In fact, in a small business environment, your CPA firm will be your closest financial advisor—closer than your attorney, broker, financial planner, or insurance agent.

Another mistake many small business owners make is trying to save a buck by doing the financial statements and/or tax returns themselves.

This is not just a mistake—it is a huge mistake.

It takes up tons of your time, time that you could be spending on developing your business, or spending with your family.

Do not fall for the advertising blitz from well-known software companies, like QuickBooks®, Peachtree®, or TurboTax®. They make it seem like it is a piece of cake to do your own books or taxes. Just click here, click there, and your financial numbers or tax return will miraculously appear and be correct.

Although they all have good products, they can also be very dangerous products. Someone with accounting knowledge still needs to get the output to be correct. It is a tool to use to get the job done. Period. Without the proper knowledge, your books or taxes will be garbage in, garbage out.

This is no different than any other field.

What if we gave you the tools to build a house, or to fix a car, or to close a real estate deal? Could you do it? You probably could muddle your way through it, but what would the outcome be?

Would it be the same output as if a professional general contractor, mechanic, or attorney had done it? We seriously doubt it. This is no different, no matter what the software company's marketing department will try to convince you of.

We can tell you from direct experience and this is the honest truth. In all the years we have been in business, we have NEVER seen a set of accounting books done with QuickBooks® or Peachtree® that has come into our office completely, 100% correct.

You heard us right. NEVER!!! Trust us. We have seen thousands of financials come across our desk, and not one was ever 100% correct. That is pretty pathetic.

Do not fall into the trap of stepping over dollars to pick up dimes. Your financial statement is one of the most important documents you and your CPA firm has to monitor your business.

It IS the cornerstone upon which you will be building your business empire.

Do not, and we repeat, do not leave this all-important task of preparing your company's financial statement up to yourself, your spouse, your neighbor, your parents, your kids, your best friend, or anyone who is not a professional accountant. Leave this task up to the professionals!!!

Why do you need financial statements?

It is impossible for you to manage your business if you don't have accurate and timely financial statements. Your financial statements should provide you with complete and pertinent data about your business at all times.

Take a look at the following example. This is like the financial statements we provide to each and every client, each and every month. Your financial statement should have a minimum of four years of comparisons, if you've been in business for that long, along with corresponding percentages for the income statement.

Financial statements should be analyzed by the percentages, in addition to the raw numbers.

Sample Client
Statement of Assets, Liabilities, and Equity - Income Tax Basis
September 30, 20XX

ASSETS

CURRENT ASSETS

Cash on Hand & in Bank	$ 104,387.09	
Total Current Assets		104,387.09

FIXED ASSETS

Fixed Assets	671,479.61	
Accumlated Depreciation	(297,723.38)	
Total Fixed Assets		373,756.23

OTHER ASSETS

Intangible Assets	539.75	
Accumulated Amortization	(526.50)	
Deposits	268.00	
Total Other Assets		281.25
TOTAL ASSETS		$ 478,424.57

LIABILITIES & STOCKHOLDERS EQUITY

CURRENT LIABILITIES

Accrued Payroll Taxes	$ 4,342.65	
Loans Payable-Current	68,227.82	
Total Current Liabilities		72,570.47

OTHER LIABILITIES

Loans Payable-Long Term	200,477.85	
Total Other Liabilities		200,477.85

STOCKHOLDERS EQUITY

Equity	10,723.97	
Net Income (Loss)	194,652.28	
Total Stockholders Equity		205,376.25
TOTAL LIABILITIES & EQUITY		$ 478,424.57

For Management Purposes Only - See Accountants' Compilation Report

1

Sample Client
Statement of Assets, Liabilities and Equity - Income Tax Basis
Supplemental Schedules
September 30, 20XX

CASH ON HAND & IN BANK DETAIL

Cash in Bank-Checking	$	98,337.90	
Cash in Bank-Payroll		6,049.19	
Total Cash on Hand & in Bank			$ 104,387.09

FIXED ASSETS DETAIL

Furniture & Fixtures	$	17,041.98	
Machinery & Equipment		574,388.46	
Automobiles		43,726.97	
Office Equipment		23,237.60	
Leasehold Improvements		13,084.60	
Total Fixed Assets			$ 671,479.61

ACCUMULATED DEPRECIATION DETAIL

A/D Furniture & Fixtures	$	(6,822.78)	
A/D Machinery & Equipment		(260,779.94)	
A/D Automobiles		(17,660.78)	
A/D Office Equipment		(11,538.88)	
A/A Leasehold Improvement		(921.00)	
Total Accumulated Depreciation			$ (297,723.38)

INTANGIBLE ASSETS DETAIL

Organization Expense	$	539.75	
Total Intangible Assets			$ 539.75

ACCUMULATED AMORTIZATION DETAIL

A/A Organization Expense	$	(526.50)	
Total Accumulated Amortization			$ (526.50)

For Management Purposes Only - See Accountants' Compilation Report
2

Sample Client
Statement of Assets, Liabilities and Equity - Income Tax Basis
Supplemental Schedules
September 30, 20XX

ACCRUED PAYROLL TAXES DETAIL

Federal Withholding	$ 3,332.79	
State Withholding	999.84	
Federal Unemployment Tax	10.02	
Total Accrued Payroll Taxes		$ 4,342.65

LOANS PAYABLE-CURRENT DETAIL

S/T-Loans Payable Haas VMC	$ 10,827.48	
S/T-Loans Payable #4 EDM	4,385.28	
S/T-Loans Payable Van	4,513.44	
S/T-Loans Payable CNC EDM #1	26,218.44	
S/T-Loans Payable CNC EDM #2	12,302.52	
S/T-Loans Payable Wire EDM	9,124.08	
S/T-Loans Payable #3 EDM	856.58	
Total Loans Payable-Current		$ 68,227.82

LOANS PAYABLE-LONG TERM DETAIL

L/T-Loans Payable Haas VMC	$ 46,241.19	
L/T-Loans Payable #4 EDM	3,154.82	
L/T-Loans Payable Van	7,100.40	
L/T-Loans Payable CNC EDM #1	36,152.66	
L/T-Loans Payable CNC EDM #2	63,605.29	
L/T-Loans Payable Wire EDM	44,223.49	
Total Loans Payable-Long Term		$ 200,477.85

EQUITY DETAIL

Common Stock	$ 1,000.00	
Previously Taxed Income	(83,114.82)	
Retained Earnings Begin	92,838.79	
Total Equity		$ 10,723.97

Sample Client
Comparative Statement of Assets, Liabilities, and Equity - Income Tax Basis

ASSETS

CURRENT ASSETS	09/30/XX	09/30/XX	09/30/XX	09/30/XX
Cash on Hand & in Bank	$ 104,387.09	69,980.07	56,996.91	11,790.67
Accounts Receivable	(0.00)	(0.00)	59,204.74	(0.00)
Total Current Assets	104,387.09	69,980.07	116,201.65	11,790.67
FIXED ASSETS				
Fixed Assets	671,479.61	563,920.38	353,612.04	163,886.07
Accumulated Depreciation	(297,723.38)	(209,958.63)	(122,499.17)	(73,415.57)
Total Fixed Assets	373,756.23	353,961.75	231,112.87	90,470.50
OTHER ASSETS				
Intangible Assets	539.75	539.75	539.75	539.75
Accumulated Amortization	(526.50)	(459.00)	(351.00)	(243.00)
Deposits	268.00	268.00	268.00	268.00
Total Other Assets	281.25	348.75	456.75	564.75
TOTAL ASSETS	$ 478,424.57	424,290.57	347,771.27	102,825.92

LIABILITIES & STOCKHOLDERS EQUITY

CURRENT LIABILITIES				
Accrued Payroll Taxes	$ 4,342.65	5,618.08	4,333.40	660.80
Loans Payable-Current	68,227.82	0.00	0.00	0.00
Total Current Liabilities	72,570.47	5,618.08	4,333.40	660.80
OTHER LIABILITIES				
Loans Payable-Long Term	200,477.85	240,820.75	127,147.02	27,307.64
Due to Officers & Sharehold	0.00	1,617.35	29,097.35	44,661.85
Total Other Liabilities	200,477.85	242,438.10	156,244.37	71,969.49
STOCKHOLDERS				
Equity	10,723.97	23,369.31	75,410.40	2,066.89
Net Income (Loss)	194,652.28	152,865.08	111,783.10	28,128.74
Total Stockholders Equity	205,376.25	176,234.39	187,193.50	30,195.63
TOTAL LIAB & EQUITY	$ 478,424.57	424,290.57	347,771.27	102,825.92

For Management Purposes Only - See Accountants' Compilation Report
4

Sample Client
Statement of Revenues and Expenses - Income Tax Basis
For the One Month and Nine Months Ended September 30, 20XX

	1 Month Ended September 30, 20XX	Percent	9 Months Ended September 30, 20XX	Percent
REVENUES				
Sales	$ 62,773.00	100.00	$ 646,318.54	100.00
Total Revenues	62,773.00	100.00	646,318.54	100.00
COST OF SALES				
Designs Expense	2,150.00	3.43	16,355.00	2.53
Direct Labor	11,188.75	17.82	120,345.47	18.62
Subcontractors	18,863.54	30.05	105,415.85	16.31
Freight	0.00	0.00	2,554.80	0.40
Supplies-Operating	1,018.70	1.62	9,103.62	1.41
Supplies-Machine	442.18	0.70	9,496.60	1.47
Payroll Taxes	855.98	1.36	9,688.94	1.50
Depreciation	9,725.31	15.49	77,055.72	11.92
Total Cost of Sales	44,244.46	70.48	350,016.00	54.16
Gross Profit	18,528.54	29.52	296,302.54	45.84
OPERATING EXPENSES				
Operating Expenses (Net)	13,692.74	21.81	84,464.54	13.07
Total Operating Expenses	13,692.74	21.81	84,464.54	13.07
Income from Operations	4,835.80	7.70	211,838.00	32.78
OTHER INCOME & (EXPENSE) ITEMS				
Interest Expense	(2,683.13)	(4.27)	(17,185.72)	(2.66)
Total Other Inc & Exp Items	(2,683.13)	(4.27)	(17,185.72)	(2.66)
NET INCOME (LOSS)	$ 2,152.67	3.43	$ 194,652.28	30.12

Sample Client
Statement of Revenues and Expenses - Income Tax Basis
Supplemental Schedule of Operating Expenses
For the One Month and Nine Months Ended September 30, 20XX

	1 Month Ended September 30, 20XX	Percent	9 Months Ended September 30, 20XX	Percent
Advertising	$ 0.00	0.00	$ 590.92	0.09
Amortization	4.50	0.01	40.50	0.01
Auto Expense	653.56	1.04	3,378.48	0.52
Bank Service Charges	50.00	0.08	87.00	0.01
Depreciation	767.72	1.22	5,952.66	0.92
Donations	50.00	0.08	589.98	0.09
Dues & Subscriptions	23.95	0.04	303.95	0.05
Employee Benefits	0.00	0.00	29.55	0.00
Entertainment	1,479.86	2.36	3,293.28	0.51
Equipment Rental	177.20	0.28	360.80	0.06
Insurance	1,977.87	3.15	9,105.41	1.41
License & Titles	0.00	0.00	221.00	0.03
Miscellaneous	0.00	0.00	217.78	0.03
Office Supplies	489.91	0.78	1,292.75	0.20
Penalties	0.00	0.00	146.99	0.02
Postage	64.00	0.10	959.15	0.15
Professional Fees	0.00	0.00	4,520.00	0.70
Promotional	0.00	0.00	1,797.49	0.28
Real Estate Taxes	1,771.24	2.82	3,542.48	0.55
Rent	2,000.00	3.19	16,000.00	2.48
Repairs & Maintenance	2,898.66	4.62	16,624.80	2.57
State Income Tax	0.00	0.00	1,243.00	0.19
Telephone	415.83	0.66	1,731.02	0.27
Travel	0.00	0.00	4,932.53	0.76
Uniform Expense	73.04	0.12	783.92	0.12
Utilities	795.40	1.27	6,719.10	1.04
Total Operating Expenses	$ 13,692.74	21.81	$ 84,464.54	13.07

For Management Purposes Only - See Accountants' Compilation Report

6

Sample Client
Comparative Statement of Revenues and Expenses - Income Tax Basis
For the Nine Months Ended September 30

	09/30/XX	Pct	09/30/XX	Pct	09/30/XX	Pct	09/30/XX	Pct
REVENUES								
Sales	$ 646,318.54	100.00	$ 535,105.33	100.00	$ 427,784.74	100.00	$ 281,818.95	100.00
Total Revenues	646,318.54	100.00	535,105.33	100.00	427,784.74	100.00	281,818.95	100.00
COST OF SALES								
Materials	0.00	0.00	2,168.47	0.41	2,781.32	0.65	11,624.73	4.12
Designs Expense	16,355.00	2.53	15,665.00	2.93	9,287.50	2.17	7,918.00	2.81
Direct Labor	120,345.47	18.62	120,661.26	22.55	102,915.07	24.06	95,632.19	33.93
Subcontractors	105,415.85	16.31	89,503.06	16.73	85,996.69	20.10	55,651.93	19.75
Freight	2,554.80	0.40	2,096.31	0.39	2,510.77	0.59	3,122.10	1.11
Supplies-Operating	9,103.62	1.41	7,081.33	1.32	8,722.02	2.04	4,137.79	1.47
Supplies-Machine	9,496.60	1.47	2,856.77	0.53	5,418.13	1.27	729.01	0.26
Payroll Taxes	9,688.94	1.50	9,706.61	1.81	9,459.44	2.21	8,655.87	3.07
Depreciation	77,055.72	11.92	52,417.30	9.80	27,036.21	6.32	20,711.57	7.35
Total Cost of Sales	350,016.00	54.16	302,156.11	56.47	254,127.15	59.41	208,183.19	73.87
Gross Profit	296,302.54	45.84	232,949.22	43.53	173,657.59	40.59	73,635.76	26.13
OPERATING EXPENSES								
Operating Expenses (Net)	84,464.54	13.07	71,898.24	13.44	57,022.22	13.33	42,308.52	15.01
Total Operating Expenses	84,464.54	13.07	71,898.24	13.44	57,022.22	13.33	42,308.52	15.01
Income from Operations	211,838.00	32.78	161,050.98	30.10	116,635.37	27.26	31,327.24	11.12
OTHER INCOME & (EXPENSE) ITEMS								
Interest Expense	(17,185.72)	(2.66)	(8,185.90)	(1.53)	(4,852.27)	(1.13)	(3,369.19)	(1.20)
Interest Income	0.00	0.00	0.00	0.00	0.00	0.00	170.69	0.06
Total Other Inc & Exp Items	(17,185.72)	(2.66)	(8,185.90)	(1.53)	(4,852.27)	(1.13)	(3,198.50)	(1.13)
NET INCOME (LOSS)	$ 194,652.28	30.12	$ 152,865.08	28.57	$ 111,783.10	26.13	$ 28,128.74	9.98

For Management Purposes Only - See Accountants' Compilation Report

7

Sample Client
Comparative Statement of Revenues and Expenses - Income Tax Basis
Supplemental Schedule of Operating Expenses
For the Nine Months Ended September 30

	09/30/XX	Pct	09/30/XX	Pct	09/30/XX	Pct	09/30/XX	Pct
Advertising	$ 590.92	0.09	$ 345.50	0.06	$ 350.00	0.08	$ 411.06	0.15
Amortization	40.50	0.01	81.00	0.02	81.00	0.02	81.00	0.03
Auto Expense	3,378.48	0.52	2,184.97	0.41	4,096.27	0.96	1,109.36	0.39
Bank Service Charges	87.00	0.01	10.00	0.00	21.49	0.01	58.09	0.02
Depreciation	5,952.66	0.92	4,372.33	0.82	4,867.96	1.14	0.00	0.00
Donations	589.98	0.09	292.00	0.05	245.85	0.06	279.86	0.10
Dues & Subscriptions	303.95	0.05	541.99	0.10	158.00	0.04	241.00	0.09
Education Expense	0.00	0.00	0.00	0.00	150.75	0.04	0.00	0.00
Employee Benefits	29.55	0.00	113.40	0.02	0.00	0.00	62.33	0.02
Entertainment	3,293.28	0.51	2,805.22	0.52	6,067.49	1.42	1,446.51	0.51
Equipment Rental	360.80	0.06	0.00	0.00	0.00	0.00	35.00	0.01
Insurance	9,105.41	1.41	10,121.30	1.89	7,312.44	1.71	7,466.52	2.65
Laundry Maintenance	0.00	0.00	0.00	0.00	0.00	0.00	20.00	0.01
License & Titles	221.00	0.03	304.00	0.06	246.00	0.06	286.75	0.10
Miscellaneous	217.78	0.03	0.00	0.00	(10.87)	0.00	0.00	0.00
Office Supplies	1,292.75	0.20	1,240.51	0.23	528.75	0.12	1,638.61	0.58
Penalties	146.99	0.02	471.57	0.09	0.00	0.00	351.63	0.12
Postage	959.15	0.15	181.25	0.03	213.15	0.05	155.10	0.06
Professional Fees	4,520.00	0.70	2,460.16	0.46	2,315.00	0.54	1,795.00	0.64
Promotional	1,797.49	0.28	140.59	0.03	0.00	0.00	0.00	0.00
Real Estate Taxes	3,542.48	0.55	3,495.04	0.65	3,379.70	0.79	3,285.62	1.17
Rent	16,000.00	2.48	14,500.00	2.71	12,400.00	2.90	9,900.00	3.51
Repairs & Maintenance	16,624.80	2.57	16,879.40	3.15	7,581.11	1.77	4,840.90	1.72
Small Tools	0.00	0.00	211.00	0.04	388.42	0.09	242.62	0.09
State Income Tax	1,243.00	0.19	482.00	0.09	212.00	0.05	13.00	0.00
Telephone	1,731.02	0.27	1,402.88	0.26	913.28	0.21	891.08	0.32
Travel	4,932.53	0.76	2,692.60	0.50	0.00	0.00	3,942.53	1.40
Uniform Expense	783.92	0.12	728.30	0.14	528.63	0.12	233.61	0.08
Utilities	6,719.10	1.04	5,841.23	1.09	4,975.80	1.16	3,521.34	1.25
Total Operating Expenses	$ 84,464.54	13.07	$ 71,898.24	13.44	$ 57,022.22	13.33	$ 42,308.52	15.01

For Management Purposes Only - See Accountants' Compilation Report
8

Sample Client

Monthly Statement of Revenues and Expenses - Income Tax Basis

For the Nine Months Ended September 30, 20XX

	January	February	March	April	May	June	July	August	September	October	November	December	Year to Date
REVENUES													
Sales	$ 121,559.20	$ 111,769.00	$ 67,866.34	$ 20,359.00	$ 47,117.50	$ 55,074.00	$ 78,528.00	$ 77,281.50	$ 92,773.00	$ 0.00	$ 0.00	$ 0.00	$ 646,318.54
Total Revenues	121,559.20	111,769.00	67,866.34	20,359.00	47,117.50	55,074.00	78,528.00	77,281.50	92,773.00	0.00	0.00	0.00	646,318.54
COST OF SALES													
Designs Expense	0.00	5,210.00	925.00	0.00	4,440.00	2,270.00	0.00	1,760.00	2,150.00	0.00	0.00	0.00	16,355.00
Direct Labor	13,608.02	13,620.00	17,204.50	14,084.75	15,101.00	10,214.75	9,793.25	14,672.55	11,148.75	0.00	0.00	0.00	120,345.47
Subcontractors	7,204.10	10,695.43	3,737.43	2,692.77	10,221.06	8,361.02	9,812.92	2,470.09	18,863.54	0.00	0.00	0.00	105,415.85
Freight	1,069.00	26.00	31.42	575.39	44.00	238.09	350.00	0.00	0.00	0.00	0.00	0.00	2,584.90
Supplies-Operating	84.51	1,208.06	1,465.67	683.39	1,259.41	1,061.79	667.46	805.43	1,018.70	0.00	0.00	0.00	8,304.62
Supplies-Machine	944.76	1,319.87	3572.9	3,273.39	1,14.05	945.25	4703.4	34.00	442.18	0.00	0.00	0.00	9,496.60
Payroll Taxes	1,047.96	1,04193	1,776.65	1,075.47	1,215.64	903.18	749.18	1,122.45	855.98	0.00	0.00	0.00	9,688.44
Depreciation	7,575.84	7,575.84	7,575.84	7,907.73	7,812.23	9,725.31	9,725.31	9,725.31	9,725.31	0.00	0.00	0.00	77,055.72
Total Cost of Sales	32,366.18	50,434.15	33,436.78	43,555.06	51,044.20	33,570.35	30,937.60	3,731.23	44,244.46	0.00	0.00	0.00	350,016.0
Gross Profit	89,193.02	61,344.85	34,429.56	(17,085.09)	(3,926.73)	16,467.67	47,590.44	46,550.27	18,528.54	0.00	0.00	0.00	296,302.54
OPERATING EXPENSES													
Operating Expense-Other	10,378.82	8,872.13	3,797.65	10,655.78	9,208.70	12,063.15	9,207.56	9,482.92	13,692.74	0.00	0.00	0.00	84,464.54
Total Operating Expenses	10,378.82	8,872.13	3,797.65	10,655.78	9,208.70	12,063.15	9,207.56	9,482.92	13,692.74	0.00	0.00	0.00	84,464.54
Income from Operations	78,814.20	52,472.72	31,631.44	(27,660.84)	(13,225.54)	7,499.82	41,392.05	37,067.35	4,835.80	0.00	0.00	0.00	211,838.0
OTHER INCOME & (EXPENSE) ITEMS													
Interest Expense	(1,291.45)	(1,753.60)	(1,496.31)	(1,785.04)	(1,023.53)	(1,691.21)	(2,170.55)	(2,092.24)	(2,083.13)	0.00	0.00	0.00	(17,185.72)
Total Other Inc & Exp Items	(1,291.45)	(1,753.60)	(1,496.31)	(1,785.04)	(1,023.53)	(1,691.21)	(2,170.55)	(2,092.24)	(2,083.13)	0.00	0.00	0.00	(17,185.72)
NET INCOME (LOSS)	$ 77,522.75	$ 50,719.12	$ 29,135.03	$ (29,446.48)	$ (14,949.07)	$ 5,858.33	$ 39,222.31	$ 34,845.11	$ 2,752.67	$ 0.00	$ 0.00	$ 0.00	$ 194,652.28

Sample Client
Monthly Statement of Revenues and Expenses - Income Tax Basis
Supplemental Schedule of Operating Expenses
For the Nine Months Ended September 30, 20XX

	January	February	March	April	May	June	July	August	September	October	November	December	Year to Date
Professional Fees	$ 0.00	$ 855.00	$ 0.00	$ 2,000.00	$ 0.00	$ 950.00	$ 0.00	$ 745.00	$ 0.00	$ 0.00	$ 0.00	$ 0.00	$ 4,520.00
Advertising	0.00	71.00	0.00	354.70	77.74	114.21	0.00	53.17	0.00	0.00	0.00	0.00	550.82
Amortization	4.50	4.50	4.50	4.50	4.50	4.50	4.50	4.50	4.50	0.00	0.00	0.00	40.50
Auto Expense	291.75	203.60	519.43	444.65	171.75	206.99	202.70	690.73	659.50	0.00	0.00	0.00	3,373.40
Bank Service Charges	0.00	0.00	0.00	0.00	0.00	37.00	0.00	0.00	50.00	0.00	0.00	0.00	87.00
Depreciation	592.00	592.00	592.00	623.73	744.13	684.42	768.42	767.72	767.72	0.00	0.00	0.00	5,952.96
Donations	0.00	249.99	0.00	120.00	65.00	0.00	44.99	20.00	50.00	0.00	0.00	0.00	809.98
Dues & Subscriptions	135.00	35.00	0.00	135.00	0.00	0.00	125.00	0.00	23.95	0.00	0.00	0.00	393.95
Employee Benefits	0.00	0.00	0.00	20.35	0.00	0.00	0.00	0.00	0.00	0.00	0.00	0.00	20.35
Equipment Rental	0.00	0.00	0.00	0.00	0.00	193.60	0.00	0.00	177.20	0.00	0.00	0.00	369.80
Insurance	857.38	857.38	0.00	208.43	857.38	1,714.76	0.00	790.36	1,957.87	0.00	0.00	0.00	8,195.41
License & Titles	48.00	0.00	0.00	50.00	105.00	0.00	0.00	18.00	0.00	0.00	0.00	0.00	221.00
Office Supplies	54.74	42.64	0.00	248.35	12.47	0.00	73.86	9.50	450.91	0.00	0.00	0.00	1,292.73
Penalties	0.00	0.00	0.00	0.00	0.00	0.00	146.99	0.00	0.00	0.00	0.00	0.00	146.99
Postage	93.58	0.00	0.00	0.00	54.00	0.00	0.00	73.57	64.00	0.00	0.00	0.00	359.15
Promotional	1,747.49	0.00	0.00	0.00	0.00	0.00	0.00	0.00	0.00	0.00	0.00	0.00	1,747.49
Rent	4,000.00	2,000.00	0.00	0.00	2,000.00	2,000.00	2,000.00	2,000.00	2,000.00	0.00	0.00	0.00	16,000.00
Repairs & Maintenance	1,433.60	1,222.33	917.14	908.75	2,135.07	1,680.35	1,670.03	2,654.23	2,838.64	0.00	0.00	0.00	18,024.80
Real Estate Taxes	0.00	0.00	0.00	0.00	0.00	1,771.24	0.00	0.00	1,771.24	0.00	0.00	0.00	3,542.48
State Income Tax	0.00	0.00	0.00	0.00	0.00	1,248.00	0.00	0.00	0.00	0.00	0.00	0.00	1,248.00
Telephone	166.73	194.67	178.49	164.18	230.59	199.91	167.49	201.03	465.93	0.00	0.00	0.00	1,751.02
Entertainment	55.00	535.00	0.00	164.00	344.42	40.00	149.00	257.00	1,470.66	0.00	0.00	0.00	3,293.20
Travel	0.00	0.00	300.00	2,444.50	1,750.04	0.00	0.00	0.00	0.00	0.00	0.00	0.00	4,893.54
Uniform Expense	102.94	137.18	76.78	72.28	0.00	144.50	72.28	111.26	73.94	0.00	0.00	0.00	793.82
Utilities	912.33	607.64	774.94	597.15	770.02	601.15	711.90	649.90	760.41	0.00	0.00	0.00	6,730.90
Miscellaneous	0.00	0.00	0.00	0.00	0.00	217.58	0.00	0.00	0.00	0.00	0.00	0.00	217.58
Total Operating Expenses	$ 11,473.82	$ 7,873.13	$ 3,752.95	$ 8,695.70	$ 9,286.70	$ 13,102.35	$ 7,227.59	$ 9,425.95	$ 17,662.21	$ 0.00	$ 0.00	$ 0.00	$ 84,345.54

10

Sample Client
Budget Report
For the One Month and Nine Months Ended September 30, 20XX

	1 Month Ended 09/30/XX	1 Month Ended Budget	Variance	Percent	9 Months Ended 09/30/XX	9 Months Ended Budget	Variance	Percent
REVENUES								
Sales	$ 62,773.00	$ 71,347.38	$ (8,574.38)	12.02	$ 646,318.54	$ 642,126.42	$ 4,192.12	(0.65)
Total Revenues	62,773.00	71,347.38	(8,574.38)	(12.02)	646,318.54	642,126.42	4,192.12	0.65
COST OF SALES								
Materials	0.00	292.52	(292.52)	(100.00)	0.00	2,632.68	(2,632.68)	(100.00)
Designs Expense	2,150.00	2,090.48	59.52	2.85	16,355.00	18,814.32	(2,459.32)	(13.07)
Direct Labor	11,188.75	16,088.83	(4,900.08)	(30.46)	120,345.47	144,799.47	(24,454.00)	(16.89)
Subcontractors	18,863.54	11,936.42	6,927.12	58.03	105,415.85	107,427.78	(2,011.93)	(1.87)
Freight	0.00	278.26	(278.26)	(100.00)	2,554.80	2,504.34	50.46	2.01
Supplies-Operating	1,018.70	941.79	76.91	8.17	9,103.62	8,476.11	627.51	7.40
Supplies-Machine	442.18	378.14	64.04	16.94	9,496.60	3,403.26	6,093.34	179.04
Payroll Taxes	855.98	1,291.39	(435.41)	(33.72)	9,688.94	11,622.51	(1,933.57)	(16.64)
Depreciation	9,725.31	6,992.04	2,733.27	39.09	77,055.72	62,928.36	14,127.36	22.45
Total Cost of Sales	44,244.46	40,289.87	3,954.59	9.82	350,016.00	362,608.83	(12,592.83)	(3.47)
Gross Profit	18,528.54	31,057.51	(12,528.97)	(40.34)	296,302.54	279,517.59	16,784.95	6.00
OPERATING EXPENSES								
Operating Expenses (Net)	13,692.74	9,574.82	4,117.92	43.01	84,464.54	86,173.38	(1,708.84)	(1.98)
Total Operating Expenses	13,692.74	9,574.82	4,117.92	43.01	84,464.54	86,173.38	(1,708.84)	(1.98)
Income from Operations	4,835.80	21,482.69	(16,646.89)	(77.49)	211,838.00	193,344.21	18,493.79	9.57
OTHER INCOME & (EXPENSE) ITEMS								
Interest Expense	(2,683.13)	(1,091.62)	(1,591.51)	(145.79)	(17,185.72)	(9,824.58)	(7,361.14)	(74.93)
Total Other Inc & Exp Items	(2,683.13)	(1,091.62)	(1,591.51)	145.79	(17,185.72)	(9,824.58)	(7,361.14)	74.93
NET INCOME (LOSS)	$ 2,152.67	$ 20,391.07	(18,238.40)	(89.44)	$ 194,652.28	$ 183,519.63	11,132.65	6.07

For Management Purposes Only - See Accountants' Compilation Report
11

Sample Client
Budget Report
Supplemental Schedule of Operating Expenses
For the One Month and Nine Months Ended September 30, 20XX

	1 Month Ended 09/30/XX	1 Month Ended Budget	Variance	Percent	9 Months Ended 09/30/XX	9 Months Ended Budget	Variance	Percent
Professional Fees	$ 0.00	$ 328.20	$ (328.20)	100.00	$ 4,520.00	$ 2,953.80	$ 1,566.20	(53.02)
Advertising	0.00	42.81	(42.81)	100.00	590.92	385.29	205.63	(53.37)
Amortization	4.50	14.27	(9.77)	68.47	40.50	128.43	(87.93)	68.47
Auto Expense	653.56	292.52	361.04	(123.42)	3,378.48	2,632.68	745.80	(28.33)
Bank Service Charges	50.00	0.00	50.00	0.00	87.00	0.00	87.00	0.00
Depreciation	767.72	585.05	182.67	(31.22)	5,952.66	5,265.45	687.21	(13.05)
Donations	50.00	35.67	14.33	(40.17)	589.98	321.03	268.95	(83.78)
Dues & Subscriptions	23.95	71.35	(47.40)	66.43	303.95	642.15	(338.20)	52.67
Employee Benefits	0.00	14.27	(14.27)	100.00	29.55	128.43	(98.88)	76.99
Equipment Rental	177.20	0.00	177.20	0.00	360.80	0.00	360.80	0.00
Insurance	1,977.87	1,348.47	629.40	(46.68)	9,105.41	12,136.23	(3,030.82)	24.97
License & Titles	0.00	42.81	(42.81)	100.00	221.00	385.29	(164.29)	42.64
Office Supplies	489.91	164.10	325.81	(198.54)	1,292.75	1,476.90	(184.15)	12.47
Penalties	0.00	64.21	(64.21)	100.00	146.99	577.89	(430.90)	74.56
Postage	64.00	21.40	42.60	(199.07)	959.15	192.60	766.55	(398.00)
Promotional	0.00	21.40	(21.40)	100.00	1,797.49	192.60	1,604.89	(833.28)
Rent	2,000.00	1,933.51	66.49	(3.44)	16,000.00	17,401.59	(1,401.59)	8.05
Repairs & Maintenance	2,898.66	2,247.44	651.22	(28.98)	16,624.80	20,226.96	(3,602.16)	17.81
Real Estate Taxes	1,771.24	463.76	1,307.48	(281.93)	3,542.48	4,173.84	(631.36)	15.13
State Income Tax	0.00	64.21	(64.21)	100.00	1,243.00	577.89	665.11	(115.09)
Small Tools	0.00	28.54	(28.54)	100.00	0.00	256.86	(256.86)	100.00
Telephone	415.83	185.50	230.33	(124.17)	1,731.02	1,669.50	61.52	(3.68)
Entertainment	1,479.86	371.01	1,108.85	(298.87)	3,293.28	3,339.09	(45.81)	1.37
Travel	0.00	356.74	(356.74)	100.00	4,932.53	3,210.66	1,721.87	(53.63)
Uniform Expense	73.04	99.89	(26.85)	26.88	783.92	899.01	(115.09)	12.80
Utilities	795.40	777.69	17.71	(2.28)	6,719.10	6,999.21	(280.11)	4.00
Miscellaneous	0.00	0.00	0.00	0.00	217.78	0.00	217.78	0.00
Total	13,692.74	9,574.82	4,117.92	43.01	84,464.54	86,173.38	(1,708.84)	(1.98)

For Management Purposes Only - See Accountants' Compilation Report
12

Sample Client

Comparative Sales

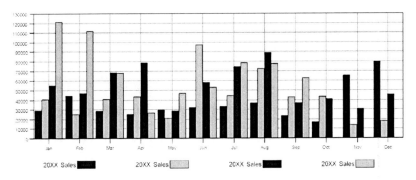

20XX Sales ▇   20XX Sales ▢   20XX Sales ▇   20XX Sales ▢

Insist that your CPA firm provide you with a four-year comparison. A two-year comparison, which most CPA firms will give you, is worthless. You read this correctly: WORTHLESS! You might as well wallpaper your bathroom with them.

Think about it for a second. For example, in a two-year comparison, if your labor or material costs last year were 22% of income, and this year, those costs are 29% of income, which percentage is correct? What if your labor dollars have increased over last year? Is that good or bad? If you only had two-year comparisons and no related percentages, you can't answer these questions. It's impossible.

Let's look at a specific example. Look at the statement on page 99, the Comparative Statement of Revenues and Expenses–Income Tax Basis (page 7 of the sample financial statement).

Are you there yet?

Let's also pretend that the numbers are your numbers for your business. Specifically, look at the Direct Labor line under the Cost of Sales section.

At first glance, a red flag and a couple of questions might come up in your head. "Why are we spending so much more on labor than we did four years ago? Four years ago, we spent $95,632 and this year we spent $120,345!! Why did we spend $25,000 more?? That must be bad, right?"

The answers to those questions cannot be answered unless you have all of the relevant data. That is why we present the data to our clients in the format shown with comparative numbers AND percentages.

In this particular case, the increase in dollars was actually a very good sign. We know you think we are crazy and saying to yourself, "How can spending $25,000 more ever be good!!"

Have faith and trust us. In this case, it is a very good thing. Let us explain. Take a closer look. Four years ago, the labor expense of $95,000 was actually 33.93 % of the revenue generated. In the current year, the $120,000 of labor spent is only 18.62 % of revenue.

Sooooo....what does that mean??

To explain it a different way: Four years ago, for every $100 of revenue the company brought in, it took $33 in labor costs to produce the product. In the current year, for every $100 of revenue brought in, it only took $18 in labor to produce the same amount of product.

In actuality, the company is almost twice as efficient in producing its product. Even though it spent $25,000 more in actual dollars, it is far better off. That is fantastic!!

Think about the flip side of this situation for a second. What if the numbers were reversed? What if it took twice the labor to produce the product today as it did last year, or four years ago. Wouldn't you want to know immediately so that you could take corrective action, Captain?

You bet your bottom dollar you would. That is why you need the financial statement on a regular *monthly* basis. Quarterly or annually just doesn't cut it. If you don't want to know, you shouldn't be at the helm running this business.

You must constantly be monitoring your expenses. Remember, *it is not what you make, it is what you keep that matters*.

You should be watching every dollar spent because it truly matters. Let's look at another example to drive this home. Turn to page 97 (page 5 of the Financial Statement.) Notice that the Net Income percentage for the nine months ended September 30 column (bottom right of the page) is 30.12 % .

So why is watching every dollar spent and this 30.12 % so important and how do they relate to each other?

Again, assume that these financials are your numbers. For giggles, let's say you are going to spend $1,000 on something. Do you realize that you will have to bring in $3,320 of revenue or sales in order for you to be able to spend the $1,000? Basically, you divide the dollar of the expense by the Net Income percentage to figure that out ($1,000 / .3012).

When you look at it from this fresh perspective, every dollar spent takes on a new meaning. It is not just a $1,000 anymore; it truly is a $3,320 effort. It is even worse if you take into account the tax consequences.

You should apply this approach to your actual numbers and percentages. Believe us, when you do, you will look at every dollar spent in a whole new light. By doing this, we guarantee you will add dollars to your bottom line.

We are going to repeat ourselves until your eyes bleed. You must constantly be monitoring your expenses. Remember, it is not what you make, it is what you keep that matters.

Got it?

Those are just a couple of examples. We could give you numerous examples from the entire financial statement.

The point is, by monitoring your financial statement numbers closely and on a timely basis, you will be able to steer the boat and turn it quickly because you will have the knowledge to do so.

Do not, and we repeat, *do not,* try to run the business blindly. Just because you have more money in your bank account this month than you did last month does not mean that you are doing better.

You have heard the phrase Knowledge is Power numerous times before. You have to have this specific knowledge in order to correct the course, if need be.

Speaking of knowledge. Has your CPA firm taught you how to read and understand your financial statement numbers? If not, insist that it shows you how. It is critical that you understand what you are looking at.

If the financials statements are formatted properly, with a little hand-holding, anyone can learn to read and apply them. You don't have to have an accounting background or be a CPA.

With the financials properly presented, it shouldn't take you more than 10 to 30 minutes per month to analyze them. Let's face it, you probably spend more time in the bathroom than that per day. In fact, your statement is a great read, so bring the financial statement and a marker with you when you go. It is a peaceful, thoughtful place where you will be undisturbed!!

If you're going to try to tell us that you can't afford the few minutes per month to be on top of your numbers, it's time for you to hang up the shingle, my friend.

This entire format is crucial to your success. You must have timely, accurate financial statements with a minimum of four years' comparison, and the corresponding knowledge of how to read them to implement any changes that need to be made.

If your CPA firm doesn't want to do this, can't do this, or tells you that you really don't need your financial statement, it's time to move on and find one that will. Get rid of that firm RIGHT NOW!!!

A great financial statement gives you the knowledge of the all-seeing Wizard of Oz. It tells you where your business has been (prior years comparative numbers), where your business is today (current monthly numbers), where your business is going in the future (analyzing and using the numbers to make intelligent future decisions).

In other words, a great financial statement is the PAST, PRESENT, and FUTURE of your business, all in a single, easy-to-read statement and all in one place.

It is a must have, can't live without, crucial document.

Quit making excuses. We don't want to hear any more of your whining. Just get it done!!!

Once you get your financial statements in order and you are reviewing them and using them in your business on a timely basis, you need to move to step two and take it to another level.

What might step two be?

Well, let's take a look.

## CHAPTER 19

WHAT ARE THE OTHER KEYS TO SUCCESS? PART II

Sooooo.....what are the other keys to success? Part II.

What else besides financial statements should you be looking at and analyzing regularly in your business?

The answer is dashboards, shown on the following pages.

Dashboards are critical and necessary for everyone in leadership roles within the company. Develop them and use them and you will bring your company to a new level.

But Tony and Frank, I don't understand. What is a dashboard and why should we develop one?

Let us explain the simple concept with an example. You know what a dashboard is in your car. Think about what it does for you. In one quick glance, you can get a reading of all the important functions of your car, from your speed, oil pressure, gas tank level, RPMs, to warning lights appearing when something isn't right.

Basically, it shows you everything important that you need to know about the running of your car in a simple, easy-to-read, quick glance.

So, why wouldn't you have something like that for your business? Why wouldn't you develop some reports that are quick and easy to read and give you the pulse of your business at regular intervals?

Having a dashboard becomes more and more important the more and more you work outside of your business— instead of working inside your business.

By reviewing the CEO Dashboard, you will be able to get the key numbers you need to make sure the business is on track without your actually being there.

However, it doesn't stop there with just the CEO Dashboard. You need to develop a dashboard for every key area within the company. Let us give you an example.

For our accounting company, we have multiple dashboards, a CEO Dashboard, a Manager's Dashboard, and a Sales Dashboard.

CEO Dashboard 20xx

20xx	January	February	March	April	May	June	July	August	September	October	November	December
Net New Accounting Clients This Month	0	0	0	0	0	0	0	0	0	0	0	0
Goal	2	2	2	2	2	2	2	2	2	2	2	2
Over (Under)	2	2	2	2	2	2	2	2	2	2	2	2
Cumulative Over (Under)	2	4	6	8	10	12	14	16	18	20	22	24
Net New Payroll Clients This Month	0	0	0	0	0	0	0	0	0	0	0	0
Goal	1.5	1.5	1.5	1.5	1.5	1.5	1.5	1.5	1.5	1.5	1.5	1.5
Over (Under)	1.5	1.5	1.5	1.5	1.5	1.5	1.5	1.5	1.5	1.5	1.5	1.5
Cumulative Over (Under)	1.5	3.0	4.5	6.0	7.5	9.0	10.5	12.0	13.5	15.0	16.5	18.0
% Clients # Processed by End of Month												
Goal	75.00	80.00	85.00	85.00	85.00	85.00	85.00	85.00	85.00	85.00	85.00	85.00
Over (Under)	75.00	80.00	85.00	85.00	85.00	85.00	85.00	85.00	85.00	85.00	85.00	85.00
% Clients $ Processed by End of Month												
Goal	75.00	80.00	85.00	85.00	85.00	85.00	85.00	85.00	85.00	85.00	85.00	85.00
Over (Under)	75.00	80.00	85.00	85.00	85.00	85.00	85.00	85.00	85.00	85.00	85.00	85.00
Total # of Incomplete Clients at EOM												
# of Incomplete - Established Clients	0	0	0	0	0	0	0	0	0	0	0	0
# of Incomplete - New Clients												
Goal for Established Clients - 10%	0	0	0	0	0	0	0	0	0	0	0	0
Over (Under) on Established Clients	0	0	0	0	0	0	0	0	0	0	0	0
% of Clients on ACH Draft	100.00	100.00	100.00	100.00	100.00	100.00	100.00	100.00	100.00	100.00	100.00	100.00
Goal	90.00	90.00	90.00	90.00	90.00	90.00	90.00	90.00	90.00	90.00	90.00	90.00
Over (Under)	10.00	10.00	10.00	10.00	10.00	10.00	10.00	10.00	10.00	10.00	10.00	10.00
% Clients Contacted												
Goal	85.00	85.00	85.00	85.00	85.00	85.00	85.00	85.00	85.00	85.00	85.00	85.00
Over (Under)	85.00	85.00	85.00	85.00	85.00	85.00	85.00	85.00	85.00	85.00	85.00	85.00
Bookkeeper Dollar per Hour												
Bookkeeper $ / Hr - Current Year - Month												
Bookkeeper $ / Hr - 1st Prior Year - Month												
Bookkeeper $ / Hr - 2nd Prior Year - Month												
Bookkeeper $ / Hr - Current YTD												
Bookkeeper $ / Hr - 1st Prior Year - YTD												
Bookkeeper $ / Hr - 2nd Prior Year - YTD												
Monthly F/S Reviewed												

20xx	January	February	March	April	May	June	July	August	September	October	November	December
Total Revenue for Both Companies												
Gross Sales - Current Month	0	0	0	0	0	0	0	0	0	0	0	0
Gross Sales - Current YTD	0	0	0	0	0	0	0	0	0	0	0	0
Gross Sales - 1st Prior YTD	0	0	0	0	0	0	0	0	0	0	0	0
Gross Sales - 2nd Prior YTD	0	0	0	0	0	0	0	0	0	0	0	0
Total Net Income for Both Companies												
Net Income - Current Month	0	0	0	0	0	0	0	0	0	0	0	0
Net Income - Current YTD	0	0	0	0	0	0	0	0	0	0	0	0
Net Income - 1st Prior YTD	0	0	0	0	0	0	0	0	0	0	0	0
Net Income - 2nd Prior YTD	0	0	0	0	0	0	0	0	0	0	0	0
Accounting Freedom, Ltd.												
Net Income % - Current YTD												
Net Income % - 1st Prior YTD												
Net Income % - 2nd Prior YTD												
Payroll Specialists, Inc.												
Net Income % - Current YTD												
Net Income % - 1st Prior YTD												
Net Income % - 2nd Prior YTD												
Business Tax Clients Completed												
# Current Year												
# 1st Prior Year												
# 2nd Prior Year												
$ Current Year												
$ 1st Prior Year												
$ 2nd Prior Year												
% Current Year												
% 1st Prior Year												
% 2nd Prior Year												
# of Personal Tax Clients Completed												
# Current Year												
# 1st Prior Year												
# 2nd Prior Year												
$ Current Year												
$ 1st Prior Year												
$ 2nd Prior Year												

The CEO Dashboard contains all of the key numbers a CEO should be looking at for our accounting firm. It contains three-year monthly and year-to-date comparatives of gross sales, net income, the number of new clients added for the month, the number of clients who dropped for the month, the percentage of completion in dollars and number, incomplete months, number and dollar of tax returns completed (business and personal), and other various items we as the CEOs want and need to look at each month.

The Manager and Sales dashboards contain all the relevant information the managers and sales personnel should be looking at for their respective departments.

Hopefully, you are getting the picture. You need to develop, maintain, and review key numbers in your business on a regular basis. This doesn't have to be cumbersome. In fact, you want it to be just the opposite.

Remember, it is a dashboard. It needs to be something quick and easy to look at, as well as comprehensive enough to give you all the key data you need in each area.

We would also suggest that, if possible, you keep these reports to one or two pages each.

Manager Dashboard 20xx

20xx	January	February	March	April	May	June	July	August	September	October	November	December
Net New Accounting Clients This Month												
Goal	2	2	2	2	2	2	2	2	2	2	2	2
Over (Under)												
Cummulative Over (Under)	2	4	6	8	10	12	14	16	18	20	22	24
Net New Payroll Clients This Month												
Goal	1.5	1.5	1.5	1.5	1.5	1.5	1.5	1.5	1.5	1.5	1.5	1.5
Over (Under)	1.5	1.5	1.5	1.5	1.5	1.5	1.5	1.5	1.5	1.5	1.5	1.5
Cummulative Over (Under)	1.5	3.0	4.5	6.0	7.5	9.0	10.5	12.0	13.5	15.0	16.5	18.0
% Clients # Processed by End of Month												
Goal	75.00	80.00	85.00	85.00	85.00	85.00	85.00	85.00	85.00	85.00	85.00	85.00
Over (Under)	75.00	80.00	85.00	85.00	85.00	85.00	85.00	85.00	85.00	85.00	85.00	85.00
% Clients $ Processed by End of Month												
Goal	75.00	80.00	85.00	85.00	85.00	85.00	85.00	85.00	85.00	85.00	85.00	85.00
Over (Under)	75.00	80.00	85.00	85.00	85.00	85.00	85.00	85.00	85.00	85.00	85.00	85.00
Average Days to Complete - Bookkeeper												
Goal	3.00	3.00	3.00	3.00	3.00	3.00	3.00	3.00	3.00	3.00	3.00	3.00
Over (Under)	3.00	3.00	3.00	3.00	3.00	3.00	3.00	3.00	3.00	3.00	3.00	3.00
Average Days to Complete - Manager												
Goal	2.00	2.00	2.00	2.00	2.00	2.00	2.00	2.00	2.00	2.00	2.00	2.00
Over (Under)	2.00	2.00	2.00	2.00	2.00	2.00	2.00	2.00	2.00	2.00	2.00	2.00
Total # of Incomplete Clients at EOM												
# of Incomplete - Established Clients	0	0	0	0	0	0	0	0	0	0	0	0
# of Incomplete - New Clients												
Goal for Established Clients - 10%	0	0	0	0	0	0	0	0	0	0	0	0
Over (Under) on Established Clients	0	0	0	0	0	0	0	0	0	0	0	0
% of Clients on ACH Draft												
Goal	90.00	90.00	90.00	90.00	90.00	90.00	90.00	90.00	90.00	90.00	90.00	90.00
Over (Under)	90.00	90.00	90.00	90.00	90.00	90.00	90.00	90.00	90.00	90.00	90.00	90.00
% Clients Contacted												
Goal	85.00	85.00	85.00	85.00	85.00	85.00	85.00	85.00	85.00	85.00	85.00	85.00
Over (Under)	85.00	85.00	85.00	85.00	85.00	85.00	85.00	85.00	85.00	85.00	85.00	85.00
Bookkeeper Dollar per Hour												
Bookkeeper $ / Hr - Current Year - Month												
Bookkeeper $ / Hr - 1st Prior Year - Month												
Bookkeeper $ / Hr - 2nd Prior Year - Month												
Bookkeeper $ / Hr - Current YTD												
Bookkeeper $ / Hr - 1st Prior Year - YTD												
Bookkeeper $ / Hr - 2nd Prior Year - YTD												
Business Tax Clients Completed												
# Current Year												
# 1st Prior Year												
# 2nd Prior Year												
$ Current Year												
$ 1st Prior Year												
$ 2nd Prior Year												
% Current Year												
% 1st Prior Year												
% 2nd Prior Year												
# of Personal Tax Clients Completed												
# Current Year												
# 1st Prior Year												
# 2nd Prior Year												
$ Current Year												
$ 1st Prior Year												
$ 2nd Prior Year												

Manager's Weekly Dashboard 20xx

For The Week Ending

	Total	Carol	Frank	Jamie	Barb	Lori	Donna	Sharon	Norman
Total Bookkeeping Completed									
# of Months	0								
Dollars	0.00								

Bookkeeping Reviewed by Manager									
# of Months	0								
Dollars	0.00								

Incomplete Months	0								

Month To Date

	Total	Carol	Frank	Jamie	Barb	Lori	Donna	Sharon	Norman
Total Bookkeeping Completed									
# of Months	0								
Dollars	0.00								

Current Month Bkkping Completed									
# of Months	0								
Dollars	0.00								
Percentage Complete #									
Percentage Complete $									

Bookkeeping Reviewed by Mgr									
# of Months	0								
Dollars	0.00								

Dashboard - Sales 20xx

20xx	January	February	March	April	May	June	July	August	September	October	November	December
New Accounting Clients This Month												
Added												
Cumulative Add	0	0	0	0	0	0	0	0	0	0	0	0
Goal												
Cumulative Goal	0	0	0	0	0	0	0	0	0	0	0	0
Over (Under)	0	0	0	0	0	0	0	0	0	0	0	0
Cummulative Over (Under)	0	0	0	0	0	0	0	0	0	0	0	0
New Payroll Clients This Month												
Added												
Cumulative Add	0	0	0	0	0	0	0	0	0	0	0	0
Goal												
Cumulative Goal	0	0	0	0	0	0	0	0	0	0	0	0
Over (Under)	0	0	0	0	0	0	0	0	0	0	0	0
Cummulative Over (Under)	0	0	0	0	0	0	0	0	0	0	0	0
Monthly Equivalent Revenue Sold - Accounting												
Added												
Cumulative Add	0	0	0	0	0	0	0	0	0	0	0	0
Goal												
Cumulative Goal	0	0	0	0	0	0	0	0	0	0	0	0
Over (Under)	0	0	0	0	0	0	0	0	0	0	0	0
Cummulative Over (Under)	0	0	0	0	0	0	0	0	0	0	0	0
Monthly Equivalent Revenue Sold - Payroll												
Added												
Cumulative Add	0	0	0	0	0	0	0	0	0	0	0	0
Goal												
Cumulative Goal	0	0	0	0	0	0	0	0	0	0	0	0
Over (Under)	0	0	0	0	0	0	0	0	0	0	0	0
Cummulative Over (Under)	0	0	0	0	0	0	0	0	0	0	0	0
Total Firm Monthly Equivalent Revenue Sold												
Added												
Cumulative Add	0	0	0	0	0	0	0	0	0	0	0	0
Goal												
Cumulative Goal	0	0	0	0	0	0	0	0	0	0	0	0
Over (Under)	0	0	0	0	0	0	0	0	0	0	0	0
Cummulative Over (Under)	0	0	0	0	0	0	0	0	0	0	0	0
Backwork & Initial Strategy Session												
Added												
Cumulative Add	3	3	3	3	3	3	3	3	3	3	3	3
Goal												
Cumulative Goal	0	0	0	0	0	0	0	0	0	0	0	0
Over (Under)	0	0	0	0	0	0	0	0	0	0	0	0
Cummulative Over (Under)	0	0	0	0	0	0	0	0	0	0	0	0
Year End Fees												
Added												
Cumulative Add	0	0	0	0	0	0	0	0	0	0	0	0
Goal												
Cumulative Goal	0	0	0	0	0	0	0	0	0	0	0	0
Over (Under)	0	0	0	0	0	0	0	0	0	0	0	0
Cummulative Over (Under)	0	0	0	0	0	0	0	0	0	0	0	0

Once you get these monitoring items working properly (financial statements and dashboards), the system will drive the business, the employees will run the system, and you will have greater knowledge and understanding of your business.

Your life will be much happier and your business will be much more profitable, eventually bringing you to the end Pot.....

What pot? We are glad you asked.

Read on! It's where you collect your reward!

CHAPTER 20

WHAT POT?

S ooooo.....what pot are we talking about???

The "Pot at the end of the Rainbow," of course... duh.

There are two possible long-term outcomes for your business rainbow. You either will have a pot full of gold at the end, or your pot will be empty. The choice is up to you.

What choices you make can have a tremendous effect on the outcome and you and your family being able to live independently wealthy or not.

Let us explain....

When you eventually decide to retire, you have two choices. You can close your business doors and be done with it, or you can sell the business to a new business owner.

Here is where it gets interesting....

If you have done all that we have suggested, have worked "outside" your business instead of "inside" it, have set up systems and procedures, have filled all of the boxes with other peoples' names, and your business runs smoothly with or without you, then you will have a valuable business asset to sell. If not, your business isn't worth nearly as much.

Think about it....

If your business is still dependent on you to produce the work and to have the client/customer contacts, you don't really have anything much to sell.

The business was you. When you go, so will the business.

If you are not there anymore, who is going to know how to do production? Are your clients/customers going to be loyal to the new owner? You get the picture.

Let us give you an actual example from our direct experience.

We are constantly looking to expand our business. Over the years, we have looked to purchase and have purchased other accounting firms. When we analyze companies to see if they will be good acquisitions or not, one of the first things we look at is the owner's role and involvement in the business.

If the owner is very involved in the daily production and client relationships, in our minds, the value of the business is substantially reduced.

The clients are used to dealing with that owner. Once the previous owner is gone, he or she will need to be replaced, and it is often difficult to transfer the client relationship to someone new. There is a much higher chance that the client will look somewhere else.

However, on the other hand, if the previous owner had set up the business properly and was working "outside" the business, the transition will be almost completely transparent to the clients.

Why is it transparent?

It is pretty simple. Clients will still be dealing with the same people (employees) they have dealt with in the past. The same manager will be meeting with them, the same bookkeeper will be doing their work, and so on.

The previous owner was just a figure head. As long as the clients are dealing with the same employees, and those employees have been treated well, they will most probably stay. It is transparent to the clients because the sale really doesn't affect them. They will be happy with whoever's name is on the door, because nothing has really changed for them.

And guess what?? When we find that type of an accounting practice, we are willing to pay a premium to get it.

What's the result?

We get a well-run accounting firm, the employees keep their jobs, the clients are still satisfied, and the previous owner gets the pot at the end of the rainbow filled with gold, and can retire independently wealthy.

It's a win-win-win-win situation for all!!

The alternative is that no one wins and everyone loses.

Your business is no different when it comes time to sell it.

What are you going to chose? Do you want a full pot of gold that allows you to retire independently wealthy, or a not-so-good alternative—an almost empty or completely empty pot?

Soooo.....what's next?

CHAPTER 21

THE LEAN, MEAN, BUSINESS MACHINE

Sooooo.....what's next?

The ultimate goal is to have a Lean, Mean, Business Machine working on all cylinders with or without your participation.

Let's summarize what we have learned so far and the steps you need to take to make this work:

- It's your fault, so get to work fixing it. Quit making excuses!

- The definition of independently wealthy is having enough income coming in to live your lifestyle without having to work

- Work "outside" the business and not "inside" it. Don't create a job for yourself.

- Working harder for less money is not the way to go.

- Go into business for the right reason, not the wrong reason. Go into business to provide work for other people.

- Are you and your business the same? They shouldn't be.

- Do not name your business after yourself. If you have already, change it.

- Make sure your business doesn't collapse and implode.

- Create an organizational chart. Fill in all the boxes with great employees.

- Set up systems that will drive the business.

- "Franchise" your business.

- The wrong way to hire and the right way to hire. Hire on the basis of work ethic, honesty, and people skills, rather than experience.

- Get the most out or your employees using your systems.

- Produce great financial statements to have the knowledge to run your business.

- Develop dashboards to give you instant snapshots of your business.

- Grab the pot of gold at the end of the rainbow when you retire or sell the business.

Having read this book, you now realize that to achieve good and consistent results, you need to dedicate sufficient time, effort, and expertise to the tasks.

However, we appreciate that time, knowledge, and expertise in these areas are resources most small business owners aren't blessed with. If you dedicate the time to implementing, learning, and generally becoming an expert in these key areas, you can achieve results.

The question we leave you with is this...

Do you have the time to do it all yourself?

If the answer is 'Yes' and you want to go through the process of trial and error, we genuinely wish you great success. You'll need it.

However, if you're like most of the business owners we meet (from start-ups to multi-million-dollar businesses), you're so busy working "inside" your business that working "outside" business, although important to you, often takes a back seat. Sure, things get done intermittently but you're constantly fighting to keep things on track. It's just not that easy.

But there is a better, proven, and easier way.

You can take the short cut to success.

You can become a client of Accounting Freedom, Ltd. or of another trusted member of the Professional Association of Small Business Accountants and immediately start to see results. (Please visit www.PASBA.org for an accountant near you.)

You see, we're different. We're not like any other firm of certified public accountants. Of course, like all good accountants, we excel at all the compliance stuff, but there are two things which really set us apart from every other firm:

First, our own expertise in running a business by working "outside" it instead of "inside" it. You've discovered just from reading this book how our expertise can help you to manage and run your business better. Few accountants are blessed with this kind of real-world expertise.

Secondly, our financial management and tax-saving expertise. We can help you with all of your accounting, payroll, and tax compliance needs, giving you total peace of mind every single day.

As you've just discovered, the combination of great knowledge and management skills and the implementation of sound financial management and tax solutions is a potent mix that leads to success.

That's why many of our clients have transformed their fortunes since joining us.

But it takes a certain kind of person and business to ensure our skills and expertise don't go to waste. For that reason, we don't meet with just anyone. Nor do we work with everyone who approaches us.

You see, to get results, the business owner(s) need to be ambitious. He or she must want to build and run a better business. In fact, the business owner must be driven to continually succeed.

Those are the people we choose to work with.

Those are the type of people who flourish.

Those are the type of people who benefit most from our services and our unique approach to accounting.

So if that's you, then we'd be delighted to meet with you or you can complete our online form at www.accounting-freedom.com.

So what are you waiting for??? Get to it and put these ideas to work and give us a call. The longer you wait, the longer you will have a business that is not profitable, and an empty pot of gold at the end of the rainbow.

You are the captain of this boat; you need to be steering it in the right direction. If you don't change, you will be like a captain in the middle of an ocean, trying to steer the boat without a rudder!!

Only when all of the points we have discussed throughout this book are in progress or have been completed, will you reach your ultimate goals:

- More profits from your own Lean, Mean, Business Machine
- More free time for yourself to enjoy those profits
- A pot full of gold at the end of your rainbow so you can retire independently wealthy!

We hope we have inspired you, put a massive fire under your butt, and opened your eyes to a whole new and exciting world of how to run a successful and profitable business.

We trust we have accomplished our goals. First, to make your business more profitable by showing you how to run it properly. Secondly, to give you more free time once your business is running properly. Lastly, to give you insights and a guide to becoming independently wealthy.

Good luck with your adventure and your journey!!

—Tony and Frank Fiore

ACKNOWLEDGMENTS

We would like to thank you for taking the time to read this book and granting us the opportunity to share our combined fifty years of accumulated knowledge in the small business arena.

Tony would like to especially thank:

My parents, Frank and Philomena, for all of the love, support, guidance, and sacrifice throughout all of the years. You have always encouraged me to be the best I can be. You have taught me the true meaning of love and family, and how important it is to cherish our Italian roots and family traditions. I love you very much.

My loving wife and best friend, Filomena, children Mena, Frank, Marisa, their spouses, Tim, Megan and Jon, and my five beautiful grandbabies, Vinny, Timmy, Mariella, Arianna, and Milena (as of this writing). Thank you for all of your love and support for all of these years. God has blessed me to be able to walk through this short period of time we spend on earth with all of you in my daily life. Without you by my side, none of this would have been worth it. All of you are my life. I could not ask for a better family. I love all of you more than life itself. Keep the grandbabies coming!!

Father Emil Agostino from Carmel High School in Mundelein, Illinois, for seeing my potential with "numbers." You started my journey by "forcing" me to take accounting classes my junior and senior years of high school, even though I didn't know what "accounting" even meant at the time.

Dave Rose and Mark Reich of Rose, Christenson and Cain, CPAs in Waukegan, Illinois, for believing in me and giving me my first accounting job out of college.

Vic Rogers from Rose, Christenson and Cain, CPAs, for being a great friend, with a great sense of humor and taking the "rookie" under your wing and teaching me more about "real world" accounting than you will ever realize.

A special thanks to Joseph Diesi, Lou Cairo, and Jay, Ron, and Roger Nally for believing in me and becoming my first clients, and for all of the clients you referred to me over the years. Without you, this journey would not have been possible.

Thanks to all of the thousands of clients who have entrusted their businesses, taxes, and investments to us throughout the years. Helping and serving you for all of these years has been an honor and a privilege. We at Accounting Freedom, Ltd, look forward to many, many more years of serving you.

My colleagues throughout the United States from the Professional Association of Small Business Accountants (PASBA) who have taught me and shared with me how to work outside of my business instead of inside it. Especially, Tom Bowman and Kim Bryant, who started the PASBA journey with me and together have helped me in more ways (business and personal) than you will ever know and that can ever be repaid. Your friendship and love will always be cherished.

David and Maria Lucier, your friendship, guidance, mentoring, wealth of knowledge, and frequent slaps upside my head when needed, have changed my life forever. You truly are like family to us, and will share our love forever.

Raymond Busch, Darlene Belter, and James Halikias (deceased), for all of the friendship, support, and consultation throughout the years.

All the members of my Financial Statement Review Group and every other member and friend in PASBA. You are too numerous to list, but have all touched me and shaped me in more ways than you can ever imagine.

Michael Arnold of Palmetto Partners, LLC, for being a good friend, sharing your knowledge, helping us grow our firm, and putting a fire under my butt to complete this book and bring it to the finish line.

All my trusted and loyal employees throughout the years. You truly have blessed me and made my life complete by helping me fulfill my dream of helping others fulfill theirs through their successful businesses. Without all of your hard work, dedication, and loyalty to me, Accounting Freedom, and our clients, none of this would have ever been possible.

Rich Haas, my partner in Payroll Specialists, Inc. You are truly a best friend and a great partner who has blessed my life in so many ways, for so many years in our personal lives, as well as in our business lives.

Jim Kruse, my partner in Accountants Solutions, Inc. Your brilliant ability to be able to write our software has helped our accounting firm and customers run their own firms more successfully and profitably. You have taught me more about life and friendship that can ever be expressed in words. You truly are one of the most honorable, kindest, gentlest men I have ever known.

Finally, thank you to my son, Frank (a chip off of the old block). It is an honor and privilege to be your father and friend, to work with you, and to have you follow in my footsteps and continue on the family business. You have worked very hard for many years working your way up through all phases of our business to become the President of our company. You have never had the sense of "entitlement," nor were you ever shown any. You have deservingly earned your way and earned the respect of our employees and clients. It is very comforting to me to know that you will be extremely successful in the future and that the business and our clients will be in very good hands. Thank you again for everything. A man could not ask for a better son. My love always, Dad.

Frank would especially like to extend his thanks:

To my wonderful family and friends who have supported me over the years. I could not have done this without you.

To my sisters, Mena and Marisa, and brother-in-laws, Tim and Jon, thank you for always being there for me throughout the years. Your encouragement and support have meant more to me then you may realize.

To my best friends John Markham, Dave Salvi, Jim Daluga, Kevin Haas, Craig Merle, and Bryan Luczkiw. You guys are the greatest group of friends I could have ever asked for. I love you all.

To all the members of PASBA. You accepted me as one of your own from the very beginning. You have taught me to not just settle for being an accountant, but to build and grow an accounting practice. A special thanks to my Financial Statement Review Group. Every year, you keep me on track to achieve my goals. It has been a privilege to learn and grow from the best minds in the business.

To all of our great clients over the years. I truly appreciate the opportunity and trust you have shown in us throughout the years. I look forward to working with you for many years to come!

To the wonderful staff at Accounting Freedom. I am honored and privileged to work with the best people around. Thank you for all your hard work and dedication over the years. We could not have done this without your support.

To my beautiful wife Megan and daughter Mariella. You have always inspired me to be the best person I can be. You have stuck by my side through the long days and nights. Thank you for being there for me. I am blessed to have such a great family. I love you both.

Last but certainly not least, I especially would like to thank my parents. I would not be the person I am today without your constant love, support, and encouragement. You have always taught me great morals and family values. I hope to be as great of a parent for my family as you are for me. I love you both.

A special thanks to my dad for giving me the opportunity to work in the family business. I could not have asked for a better mentor, teacher, and friend. I truly appreciate your hard work and dedication over the past 33 years to build the business to where it is today. You are one of the smartest business owners I know and I look forward to continuing to learn from you in the years to come.

About Accounting Freedom, Ltd.
How to Contact the Authors

Telephone: 847.949.8373
E-mail: info@accountingfreedom.com
tony@accountingfreedom.com
frank@accountingfreedom.com

Mail: Accounting Freedom, Ltd.
469 N. Lake Street
Mundelein, Illinois 60060

Website www.accountingfreedom.com

CPSIA information can be obtained
at www.ICGtesting.com
Printed in the USA
FFOW05n0448111214